# THE MIDNIGHT HOUR

# THE MIDNIGHT HOUR

*A Jungian Perspective on*
*America's Current Pivotal Moment*

## BUD HARRIS, PHD

DAPHNE PUBLICATIONS, AN IMPRINT OF SPES, INC.

Harris, Clifton T. Bud
The midnight hour: a jungian perspective on america's current pivotal moment / Bud Harris.

ISBN: 978-0-578-63261-2  Nonfiction
1. Democracy 2.Civics and Citizenship 3. Jungian psychology

Library of Congress Control Number: 2016908974
Spes, Inc, Asheville, NC

Cover and Interior Design: Courtney Tiberio

*For my grandsons: Galen and Ben*

# CONTENTS

*America's opportunity is at hand. We can lead the world by being a great example, we can prove this nation a living, growing thing with policies that are adequate to new conditions. In a thousand ways this is our hour of test... chiefly let our aim be to build up, not to tear down. Our opposition is to the things which once existed, in order that they may never return. We oppose money in politics, we oppose the private control of national finances, we oppose the treating of human beings like commodities, we oppose the salon-bossed cities, we oppose starvation wages, we oppose rule by groups or cliques. In the same way we oppose a mere period of coma in our national life.*

*—Franklin Delano Roosevelt*

*... But history will judge you, and as the years pass, you will ultimately judge yourself on the extent to which you have used your gifts to enrich the lives of your fellow man. In your hands, not with presidents or leaders, is the future of your world and the fulfillment of the best qualities of your own spirit.*

*—Robert F. Kennedy*

# AUTHOR'S NOTE

This is the third edition in which I discuss our country's current political situation. This unfolding thought process examines the chaotic political period we are experiencing as a nation and how to understand it, the effect our political choices today will have on our future, and how personal and political ideals are tightly bound in American society.Building on my earlier editions, in this volume I seek to create order out of chaos and develop a vision for the future in the crucible of my own understanding.

The 2016 presidential campaign and election were a great shock to me, though not a total surprise. I had been aware of the growing shadow in our society for a long time. But I was reluctant to face the shadow head on as well as the demands with which it was confronting us as citizens in a democracy. Our political chaos has continued as I have continued to write.

Writing is my process of bringing order out of chaos. It helps me focus on understanding my experiences, my life, what is happening to me and around me. My emotions have been aroused, and as part of this writing project I want to understand why. This awareness is crucial because my emotions tell me when my boundaries have been violated as well as when my life has been turned upside down. Emotions reveal my most profound values and ultimately, no matter how rational I believe I am, they are the power behind my decisions. It is important to include them in this writing process because they make my life real and the process encompasses a great deal more than simply seeking solutions. In addition, the emotions I have failed to face and integrate all too often become the driving force behind my temperament, health and decision making.

Whether you agree with me or not I hope my work helps you clarify your own position, both within and to the chaotic times surrounding us. Above all I hope it helps you create a new vision of the future and a new hope that draws you to commit to it.

Bud Harris
Asheville, North Carolina

*Introduction*

# WELCOME TO
# THE CHALLENGES OF CHANGE

*Change is the process by which the future invades
our lives, and it is important to look at it closely,
not merely from the grand perspective of history,
but also from the vantage point of the living,
breathing individuals who experience it.*
— Alvin Toffler, *Future Shock*

It always strikes me with awe that whether in nature, in my personal experience, or in our collective experience, life is continuously in a state of becoming. The metaphor for this process in myth and religion is life, death, and rebirth. Plants die and grow again. So do the cells in my body. The seed must die for the plant to break free and begin to sprout. Psychologically, I meet that cycle in my progressing life by going through the emotional challenges and often the pain of dying to my comfortable way of life. This may include giving up my old perspectives or my old expectations, and may require questioning my value system and the obligations it supports. Meanwhile I am caught betwixt and between while the future is invading my life. It can be scary and threatening to be in the process of becoming a new self and creating a new story or narrative that expands me, brings together my disparate parts into a cohesive whole, and gives me a new stake in life.

The reality of always becoming, always facing change hasn't fit in very well with either my ideals or plans for the future, so I have the difficult choice of either living this reality, as the great German poet Goethe wrote:

> And so long as you haven't experienced this:
> to die and so to grow, you are only a troubled
> guest on the dark earth.

Or rejecting it. However, rejecting it often means rigidifying, denying being fully alive, and at a profound level closing my heart to greater loves and creative potentials. *Hold on to old defenses*

\* \* \* \*

Most of you are well aware that the future will invade our lives with crises or turning points many times. Every significant crisis is a turning point, a moment of truth for us to face. Every such turning point requires us to make personal changes in order to resolve it satisfactorily. Successful outcomes require acceptance of our situation, self-examination, courage, a new creative vision, and action. Our country also has a national character, a social character that faces similar crises and turning points. Because our country's social character is a combination of the personalities of all of its citizens, each one of us contributes to how the crises develop, how we face and understand them, and how they are resolved. To think otherwise is to abandon the value of our citizenship in this democracy, to become subject to the forces dominating our government. If we abandon the responsibility of our citizenship, whether through frustration or through lethargy, we are abandoning the soul of our nation as it was expressed in our Declaration of Independence.

To show how our personal psychology and our social character are intertwined in the development of the crises/turning points in our nation, I will use stories from my own and others' personal experiences. I will also be using the Jungian perspective that our symptoms—the chaos, anger, and divisions we are experiencing—are symptoms from the suffering soul of our nation. These symptoms churn in our national shadow and demand that attention be paid to the harmful activities that wound our national character. Anger and pain are symptoms that call for healing and action. They are a wake-up call from our national soul that is trying to renew our relationship and commitment to the deep truths our country was founded upon.

*    *    *    *

The Jungian approach to healing divisions begins with confronting ourselves and our shadows, the realities, thoughts, and emotions we have denied and repressed. On a national level, facing our reality means that in spite of the statistics of economic success and low unemployment, too many of us are living in ways that leave our deepest needs denied and unsatisfied. Robert Kennedy summed up these points beautifully when he said, "...the gross national product does not allow for the health of our children, the quality of their education or the joy of their play. It does not include the beauty of our poetry or the strength of our marriages, the intelligence of our public debate or the integrity of our public officials. It measures neither our wit nor our courage, neither our wisdom nor our learning, neither our compassion nor our devotion to our country. It measures everything in short, except that which makes life worthwhile."

In other words, too many of us see our desire for personal and economic safety, as well as our hopes and dreams, slipping beyond the horizon. So, the crisis we are in is not just a political one. While the political one is crucially important, it is in reality the severe symptoms of a much deeper "dis-ease" swimming below the surface of our apparent affluence like a great white shark. This shark is ripping us apart from within. It is a cold devouring power and greed-driven force that has no empathy for our well-being. It dismisses imagination, thought, and foresight. It brands the passion for truth, knowledge, and civility as irrelevant.

As I ask myself how to explain this chaos and our challenge, I know I cannot just do it as an observer because I am a participant in this drama, whether I like it or not. My religion and my profession tell me there is a structural process for confronting myself, accepting reality, taking self-responsibility, and reconciling within myself and with my fellow citizens. The same process works for groups. It begins when I carefully search into my emotions, review my history and take responsibility for what I have felt, what I have done, what I have failed to do, and how I have not allowed my emotions to inform me of the reality in which I am participating. Then I must promise to do my best not to do injuries again; I must not fail to prevent them or fail to be aware of the injuries happening around me. This process is a demanding one that I kept in mind as I wrote this book.

As you read, please join me in my efforts, whether you

agree with me or not. If you don't agree with me, I hope my explanations will help you clarify your own thoughts. Unless we, as citizens, marshal the courage and humility to carry out this process of reconciliation and renewal, take action, and live in a new way, we will continue to live in denial. And to live in denial is to live a lie.

Let's be honest with ourselves. We have known at some level for decades the times in which we live have been becoming more difficult. In fact, they have been getting more difficult than many of us would like to admit. For several generations it has been hard for too many of us to talk about or even admit to ourselves the truly threatening problems in our society, institutions, and structures. We even dance around our problems at family gatherings and friendly social events because so much fear and anger are often close to the surface— closer than how to restore hope in our collective future.

We don't even have to take off our rose-colored glasses to see that anxiety, depression, addictions, suicides, divorces, and other symptoms of our stress-driven lives have become epidemic. No matter how high the stock market goes or how low the unemployment rate drops we know somewhere deep in our souls we are failing to cope with the fragmentations and fear permeating our existence. Imagine, though, that these symptoms represent our future challenging us to wake up and face the sources of this pain in our society. That is, the sources of the pain that causes the despair, anger, fear, violence, and divisions in our country.

Shouldn't waking up lead us into the healing process of reconciliation with ourselves and our fellow citizens? Don't we know the future belongs to those who are passionate and work hard on it? Isn't this the path for re-creating our lives, restoring our faith in ourselves, and renewing the values our country was founded upon—freedom, equality and opportunity for all?

## The Choice is Ours

The harsh truth is that one of our greatest difficulties is being able to look beyond our economic achievements and material success and to look inward and ask ourselves how satisfying our lives really are. We have repressed, and I think actually fear, the capacity to look at ourselves and our society with emotional honesty. By refusing to look beneath the surface in our lives we are avoiding more than our potential pain. We are also denying history's challenge to change, to allow the old ideals of the "good life" and its outlived identity structures to die while facing the struggles, commitments, and creative demands of helping new ideals form. We have reached the point where changing ourselves individually is only the beginning.

It is time for us to face these challenges and turn aside from the search for easy answers. The answers needed today require our change and growth. We must come together for the sake of our children, grandchildren, and great-grandchildren to change our world for the better. Because we have been on the wrong path too long, gradual or incremental changes are not enough. Now is the time to make fundamental, creative, and well-thought-out changes in our political and social structures to reflect how we respect and care for each other.

The dark angel of our future has seized us, just as Jacob was seized when he was forced to struggle throughout the night in the Old Testament story. Well, that dark angel has grabbed me now, and my struggle and its results are in the following pages. It has also grasped us all, whether we like to admit it or not. And, as I am a participant in our larger drama, I will face intense amounts of my own and our collective fear, anger, and frustration before seeking solutions to them as I write. Dr. Jung, who was a very thoughtful man, reminded us that, "There is no birth of consciousness without pain." And, "Emotion is the chief source of consciousness. There is no change from the darkness to light or from inertia to movement without emotion." We are all challenged, and every voice must count. Will we remember that, like Jacob, we are fighting for our lives and the future?

\* \* \* \*

Freedom from fear comes when we fully invest ourselves in the national culture, which ultimately is the foundation for our identities, finding our meaning or life purpose, and our sense of community. Writing this message-driven memoir shares my shocks, my rage, and my pain. The depth of those emotions comes from confronting my shadow as a contributing participant in our great political drama as it unfolds around us. It also led me back into our history, helping me realize the potentials for facing the future that are in our heritage.

Confronting my shadow has been intense work because I have been peeling back the layers of my own feelings, seeking the deeper truths about who I am. The harsh reality is that it took the shock of national politics in 2016 - 2017 to break through the surface crust of my indoctrination of being positive and thinking the best decisions are made when emotions are suppressed. But a boil must be lanced and the infection drained in order for healing to begin. In addition, it turns out that our emotions are crucial factors if we are to make decisions about pursuing actions based on our values. They inform us about what we really value. So, it is better for us to be fully aware of them than to repress them. I was surprised at the strength of the emotions I uncovered. And, just to note, we become vulnerable to fanaticism, ideologies, and scape-goating when our emotions are repressed and denied enough that we are blind to them and the values they are crying out for us to acknowledge.

The only sure road into a positive, life-giving future is to accept our reality and our failures today, and to face the challenges they reveal. The good news is that entering fully into that arena creates a culture that supports and fosters life instead of smothering it with fear, stress, and resentment. This is worth our dedication.

# PART I

---◆◆---

## The Challenge of
## Turning Change into Opportunity

*Efforts and courage are not enough without purpose and direction.*

—*John F. Kennedy*

*Nearly all great civilizations that perished did so because they had crystallized, because they were incapable of adapting themselves to new conditions, new methods, new points of view. It is as though people would literally rather die than change.*

—*Eleanor Roosevelt*

# ONE

─────◆┼◆─────

# THE REBIRTH OF HOPE

*I call heaven and earth as witnesses today against*
*you, that I have set before you life and death,*
*blessing and curse: therefore, choose life, that*
*both you and your descendants may live.*
                                        —*Deuteronomy 30:16*

Too many people would love for us to lose heart
and believe these times are hopeless, that we
have no power and therefore little reason to
act. Do you remember that our nation began in a time
when there was a crisis of faith, despair, and conflict?
Our own history teaches us not to throw hope away
because it is meant to be reborn during our darkest hours. Our challenge as Americans is to face ourselves and reclaim the heart of our republic. Our challenge is to bring forth a new day, a total change in our
perspective and in the reality of how we are living as
citizens. This book is my effort to recognize an unexpected,
nightmarish time as an extraordinary transformation-
al moment. More often than not, such moments are

rooted in shocking events, conflict, fear and anger. But if we can accept these dark moments and look through them, the path toward a new vision of life will unfold.

One of the most difficult aspects of converting change into opportunity is fully accepting our reality. This book is my impassioned effort to look in the mirror to see our social reality as I have experienced it—including its dark side that too many of us have denied—and to initiate ideas for change. Believe me, if we don't become partners in initiating the changes knocking on our doors, they will kick our doors open. Then they will force us to pay a higher price than was originally asked of us.

At the stroke of midnight, noon is born. At the darkest hour of the night, the approach of a new day begins, and there is evidence for hope. Yet I know all too well that before we get a glimmer of light, there is darkness, both in the approach to the turning point and after it. The presidential election of 2016 was a midnight hour for me, and I wrote this book as part of my struggle through the bewildering pre-dawn hours of concern for the state of affairs in our nation. As I wrote and struggled with my experience and our reality, I became convinced that we must not lose heart but rather answer the call. The call of the future is to redress our failures to act and to acknowledge our blindness to our social problems— including the large numbers of fellow citizens who are suffering, being hurt and dehumanized by the character of our society. But, even more than that, I had to face my denial of how I was being damaged and dehumanized, and so were my children and grandchildren.

I was raised, and raised my children, in a culture where denial came all too easy. The artful denial of problems and of the crying need for changes was coupled with a persona that reflected a rigid maintenance of a positive attitude. This combination only strengthens our problems and fills them with a power that is unseen until it explodes in our faces. It is more obvious than I like to believe that we naturally tend to avoid delving into the complexity, emotional impacts, and confusion of problems calling for major changes. Seeking to penetrate and understand the roots of problems demanding real change, whether personal or societal, requires all of the powers of our hearts and minds. For this very reason you may find some of this book as hard to read as I found it to write. Facing the fact that we citizens have been asleep at the wheel of our democracy for decades without realizing it is as bitter as midnight is dark. But it is the first step toward a new day.

Today is our time in history. This is our quest, the challenge the future has put in front of us. It is also a time for us to remember the great heritage which is our strength. Our nation, America, has had the ability to stand up to any challenge, no matter how difficult it has been. It is time for us to be engaged, to be in the arena with heart and soul.

The opening chapters of this book reflect the experiences of my midnight hour. Clearly, I am not writing to bash any candidate or political party. The rage and shame I express are symptoms of the deeper issues I want to face. My concerns begin with looking into my rude awakening to the disappointment, meanness, cruelty, violence, and indifference that lie behind the prosperous façade of the society we have created. Accepting this reality lays the foundation for a new path into the future. I openly share the rage and shame that come from facing my part, my blindness, in helping to create this society. My hope comes from our heritage, our potentials for change, and the solutions I present and discuss.

As I was writing, I used my experience in living for over eight decades—my life as a Jungian psychoanalyst, writer, and lecturer—my years of working in business—my time as a volunteer in inner-city poverty areas—my participation in our repressive, positive-thinking zeitgeist—and as a member of a cross-generational family ravaged by a warped health and mental health care system—to trace how over the decades we Americans have veered from our country's highest values of democracy, liberty, equality, and opportunity for all toward indifference, blindness, and overbearing self-interest.

In this book I am very clear that I am no enemy of capitalism. But I am a critic of the heartless capitalism and predatory power structures we feel too weak to oppose. As we learn how to confront ourselves and answer the call of the future, we can rediscover our power in the heart of our democracy. When our past and our reality are seen clearly, the vision can release us and become a torch lighting the way into a new day. We can change our world because that possibility is built into the U.S. Constitution, and we have changed the world many times before. Now is the time for us to step into the challenges of the future.

# TWO

— ◆ —

# AWAKENING AT MIDNIGHT

*Sooner or later, we are each called to face what we fear, respond to our summons to show up, and overcome the vast lethargic powers within us. This is what is asked of us, to show up as the person we really are, as best we can manage, under circumstances over which we may have no control.*
—*James Hollis*

Twin demons - fear + lethargy

I hated thinking about writing this book as much as I hated thinking about the election that made it necessary. And as much as I hated enduring the emotions I felt while writing it, Melusina, that flaming bitch of a muse that lives in some dark interior cavern of my soul, wouldn't let me rest. Although I resisted, she wouldn't let me alone. When I least expected it, she would lash me with ideas, rage, and despair at the shame of my own prior blindness. So, I finally surrendered, bit the bullet, began listening to her in earnest, and began writing, began speaking the truth to myself that I have resisted for so long.

She urged me to see beyond my daily shock and disgust with our politics and to return to the roots of my Jungian perspective—to search out, once again, the writers, teachers, and speakers who have contributed so much to my life. She knew, before I remembered, that their vision, courage, and dedication to making our lives better and more whole is contagious. I have been re-reading them, listening to them, and absorbing them into my heart in new ways.

For example, when re-reading a piece by Sir Laurens van der Post, I was stunned when I read this question: "Has there ever been another age that, knowing so clearly the right things to do, has so consistently done the wrong ones?" It succinctly echoed my own thoughts. After this election and the events leading up to it, covering decades, I have spent many hours reflecting on what my part in all this tumult has been.

*   *   *   *

The difficulty and loneliness of writing this book was lightened by listening to lectures, talks, and speeches by Carl Jung, Martin Luther King Jr., Elie Wiesel, Maya Angelou, Robert Kennedy, and a varied list of others. Their courage, love, and vision represent the flame of the American spirit that has called out to me over my eight decades of living.

As I listened to these recordings, some of which are very old, I sometimes sank into reverie. For example, imagine presidential candidate Robert Kennedy standing on the back of a flatbed truck at night speaking to a crowd of poor black inner-city residents on one of the darkest nights of the soul in our time—the night Martin Luther King Jr. was assassinated. Imagine him speaking, against the advice of the Indianapolis mayor and police chief not to do so, and joining the people in their shock and grief...and moving them to join him in the quest for peace. Imagine him quoting the ancient Greek poet Aeschylus, saying, "And even in our sleep, pain which cannot forget falls drop by drop upon the heart, until in our own despair, against our will, comes wisdom through the awful grace of God." Imagine him asking them to join him in taming "the savageness of man" and making gentle the life of this world. He closed by asking that we say a prayer for our country and for our people. How I long for a spirit like that, to find it within myself!

So there I was, listening and beginning to write, hoping to find a spark in the ashes of the American spirit that could be formed into a new flame, or more important, perhaps, to find a spark in the ashes of my own public spirit that could be rekindled.

The usual negative voices that come when I am writing popped up here and there, and one said, "You're not a politician, a social scientist, or a social commentator. Who do you think you are to be writing this?" I answered "I am one who cares deeply about this country and the spirit that has so far arisen out of its darkest hours. It is the spirit that close friends and family members have fought and died for. It is the spirit that has nourished and inspired parts of my best self, and I care deeply about this spirit living into the world of my children, their children, and their children's children."

I know very well that nothing can be changed until it is accepted, experienced, defined, understood, and then acted upon. We cannot become responsible for something we do not admit we have. With these thoughts in mind, I began to write. As I wrote, I wanted to face reality, to seek new understanding, and to fan a new flame within myself and within you. For us to accomplish real change, this flame must come alive in me and you. In reality, essential change can never depend on a candidate or a political party. It must begin in the individual and grow outward.

\* \* \* \*

The work of Dr. Jung has inspired and supported my life for over fifty years. During this current, unsettling period, I have done my best to restore my basic approach to his work and to human development as one that values the whole person, the individual. Now I broaden that perspective to encompass the growth, development, and difficulties facing our nation's social character.

Dr. Jung helps me understand this perspective. The general theme in the Jungian approach is to face the transitional periods, crises, challenges, and problems in our lives as opportunities—actually, demands. This allows us to grow and enlarge who we are in order to live with more hope and satisfaction and discover new defining principles to guide us. Otherwise, we shrink into a state of defensive encapsulation. Dr. Jung emphasizes the need to experience our lives fully, to let meaning penetrate us thoroughly through feeling, thinking, and acting. The process goes something like this: fully engage in and experience life, reflect upon experiences and seek to understand them, bear the burden of conflicts that come up in this process, and then act on them. This enables us to live so that our lives are an expression of our expanded personalities, our self-awareness, and our purpose. In order to allow the emergence of a new version of our lives, the process often calls us to go back through the thickets of old memories that continue to shape us.

As I face, struggle, flounder, and go through these periods in my life, I am reminded of the writings of Thomas Wolfe (a well-known writer from Asheville, my hometown) and his novel *You Can't Go Home Again*. The book reveals a deeper meaning in its title. As life progresses, it suggests, we go through transitional periods where we can no longer blindly depend upon the social, economic, and ethical structures in our past to carry us into the future. In every transition in our lives, we will go through a period of feeling inner "homelessness." I have been shocked into such a place. I have been in that place since the election and am still emerging from it.

In writing this book, I have pursued this quest into our collectively denied realities. No longer can I hide in my illusions of being preoccupied with my own life. I have had to confront new areas in my shadow of rage, despair, disgust, and disappointment—my "inner deplorables." I have had to face many uncomfortable truths. I have had to look in the mirror and confess that our politics and our government reflect the state of our collective soul. The election of 2016 must shake the very foundation of our conscience.

I have been forced to probe more deeply into the problems of being human in our society than I initially wanted to. I invite you to do the same thing, so that together we can work to change our country and our politics and, therefore, our lives -- for the better. All my experiences teach me that facing the reality of our darkness enables us to discover how its energy can become a force for light.

# THREE

# THE CHALLENGE TO CHANGE DESTRUCTION AND RE-CREATION

*The most intense conflicts, if overcome, leave behind a sense of security and calm that is not easily disturbed. It is just these intense conflicts and their conflagration which are needed to produce valuable and lasting results.*

—*C.G. Jung*

Exploding in fire and ice marks the end of the world of gods and men according to the old Norse storytellers. They are right. When I awakened the morning after the 2016 presidential election, my world view had been blown to pieces—destroyed by the fires of fury and the ice of despair. Ragnorak, the Twilight of the Gods, the legendary myth of the world ending in fire and ice, presents breathtaking images that portray how I felt on that morning and for many days after. These powerful images illustrate how the principles, beliefs, perceptions, and, yes, the fictions that I had structured my life upon were suddenly annihilated in an inner holocaust brought on by events. I was left frozen and stunned.

The end of the world left little hope for the future in Norse mythology. But the archetypal pattern of life is destruction and creation. In the Norse tradition, creation isn't so easy either, and it also occurs in ice and fire. The sturdy members of this old tradition abandoned naïve hope and placed their aspirations on heart—being fully engaged in the struggles of life, in living intensely in the midst of blood, sweat, tears, and laughter.

*     *     *     *

Melusina has driven me back into the fray of our collective life after the year-long nightmare preceding the election and my subsequent months of being shell-shocked and just wanting to ignore it all.

Later in the morning after the election, I heard the shock and tears in my daughters' voices. In spite of all that has followed I cannot forget those moments. These conversations still haunt me and make me think deeply about the world I helped to create for them and their children to live in. As my day progressed, I heard many more voices expressing shock and dread, especially the voices of women, but of men too. They shared their surprise and fear with me, anxious to be heard. Many of our illusions about our society were being shattered as ignorance, coarseness, bullying, misogyny, and bigotry swept across the internet and through the media, invading our homes and our souls. Ugly acts of violence, prejudice, gay bashing, and life threats took place in our small town as if this kind of behavior was now sanctioned. Progress toward economic and social fairness, and toward culture, justice, and compassion in our health care system seemed to have been stabbed in front of our faces.

But not everyone reacted this way. Some experienced new hope, feeling like they had made a difference and that their voice had finally been heard. And more of these people than I would have initially imagined were affluent and educated. While I have been reflecting on what this election is trying to tell us, I have come to realize why so many of us have a deep anger toward our government, and the false promises of our politicians. Too many of us feel that our government has had no interest in our well-being for decades. All too often I have heard people say things like, "our government wants to give you nothing and take, take everything away," or "it wants to take over our lives."

This election was not my first experience of fire and ice in a society turned upside down by fury, dread, and darkness. As a young southern man, a little over fifty years ago, I was awakened in the midst of another social nightmare that ended my life as I had known it. The ugly response of some people in the South to the civil rights movement left me outraged and traumatized. The fury, the cruelty, and the brutality shown by many of the people I had grown up with was disheartening. These were my neighbors, school friends, fellow church members, and people who had brought dishes of food to our home after my mother's death when we were young. They were the policemen, mayors, governors, congressmen, and senators whom I had been raised to respect. My world view ended in fire and ice. I have never recovered from that shock and don't trust the dark undertow in the shadow of our social character.

Nightmares, whether societal or personal, have a purpose. Sometimes they are trying to wake us to the truth of what we are experiencing. Sometimes they are trying to help us absorb the emotional impact of traumas we have lived through. And sometimes they are trying to alert us to the illusions we have been living in and make us aware of the depth of pain and frustration in our lives—feelings that we have been stubbornly denying and trying to remain indifferent toward. These nightmares from the depth of our souls call us to find a new approach to life. How to recognize and accept the social wastelands we've created and how to midwife new creation and hope from their darkness are deep concerns for me as I write.

## Hope in the Dark

These same nightmares can also be seen as light-bringers, launching us on a new creative journey. Destruction in fire and ice actually calls for a new force of creation that will redeem our situation. Nightmares, whether sleeping or waking, whether personal or societal, are telling us that powerful forces are moving within and around us that we have been denying. If we can struggle into awareness and seek to understand the meaning behind our nightmares and the emotions they arouse, we can begin to see the extraordinary demands for change confronting us and the opportunities behind them. A collective nightmare that is trying to awaken us to our national reality initially seems like the end of the world as we have known it because it is. Of course, the experience is scary and demoralizing. But like personal nightmares, these experiences, these waking dreams, are meant to confront our complacency and indifference and to awaken our hearts and our courage. It is easy to say a candidate appealed to the worst in our social character. It is just as easy to displace our shock by reducing the opposing candidate and his or her followers to a shadow projection of our own expressed in psychobabble.

Blaming candidates, their parties, and their followers may have some validity and will surely fuel our outrage. But this approach can also subtly increase our defeatism, cynicism, amnesia, and feelings of hopelessness. Our opponents love for us to take this last position and to feel like we are powerless, and our actions aren't worth the trouble because they won't make any difference. It might be more accurate to suggest that the candidate or party appealed to the rage, fear, alienation, and helplessness that were dammed up in our collective shadow and erupted in the face of our denial.

These eruptions remind us that we must courageously look in the mirror, examine our own shadows, and begin living more vigilantly and realistically. A realistic outlook will remind us that there never is a permanent happy ending to life's stories, and there never was a so-called golden age of greatness and smooth sailing in our past. It is far better for us to remember that it is our courage, our awareness, and the living and evolving manner in which we face our challenges that are more important than dreaming of wishful happy endings and positive outcomes.

It took me a few decades to learn that life is a flow of creation, destruction, and re-creation. When we are in the destruction phase, we often feel stuck, life seems chaotic, out of control, threatening and even despairing. In reality we are being faced with a turning point. We are being challenged to choose between regressing and re-creating. It took me a bit longer to learn that happiness, joy, and fulfillment are not goals to be achieved. They are the result of being fully engaged in the blood, sweat, tears, fears, love, and laughter of real life. True peace of mind comes from having the will and courage to confront the darkness and uncertainties we are facing and heal the splits within our unconscious shadows, both personal and cultural—the things we have closed our eyes and ears to.

## Destruction and Re-Creation

The aftermath of this election opened the door of my psyche to the two-o'clock-in-the-morning questions that wake me up and haunt me until I overcome my inertia, pay attention to them, and struggle to answer them. The questions came. "What in the world is happening to us? How can I understand what's happening on a more realistic and profound level? What kind of radical changes is destiny calling us to undertake?"

I am well aware that the pursuit of a higher purpose is one of our often unrecognized or denied instinctual needs, and our failure to face and fulfill it lies in the center of every experience of destruction that is calling for re-creation. Shock, rage, despair, failure, and stagnation always open the door to this instinctual spiritual need in the midst of our daily lives. Freedom from fear, like peace of mind, begins with being willing to confront the darkness and search for its source.

# PART II

## Understanding and Healing Divisions

*Knowing our own darkness is the best method for dealing with the darkness of other people. One does not become enlightened by imagining figures of light, but by making the darkness conscious. The most terrifying thing is to accept oneself completely. Your visions will become clear only when you can look into your own heart. Who looks outside, dreams; who looks inside, awakes.*

—Carl Jung

# FOUR

# THE CREATIVE POWER IN FACING OURSELVES

*If I admit with Richard Wright in that poem "Between the World and Me" that evil goes into me as does the good, then I'm obliged to study myself, to center myself and make a choice. For I must know that the battles I wage are within myself. The wars I fight are in my mind. They are struggles to prevent the negative from over-taking the positive, and to prevent the good from eradicating all the negative and rendering me into an apathetic, useless organism, which has no struggle, no dynamic, and no life.*

—*Maya Angelou*

The shock of the election and the traumatic stress-inducing political chaos that has followed it has left me aware that a much larger portion of my fellow citizens than I knew are strangers to me. Thinking about this realization and the darkness around this election brought to mind a frightening story I read in my childhood.

Do you remember the story by Robert Lewis Stevenson about a fatal split in a man's personality titled *The Strange Case of Dr. Jekyll and Mr. Hyde*? Though I didn't realize it at the time, this book was telling me exactly how I could be creating my life in a "bubble" by trying to build a good and thriving life by conventional standards and at the same time create a dark shadow—my inner deplorables. While Dr. Jekyll was devoting himself to living a life he believed was admirable, useful, and safe, he was denying and repressing significant aspects of himself in order to do so. In fact, we all are indoctrinated to think, feel, and behave in certain ways to fit in, feel safe, and attempt to thrive within our families and social groups.

Even in the best of circumstances, our norms are made up in general of our social group values, our parents' biases, and characteristics that are often ordinary and mundane. We can imagine Dr. Jekyll trying to have a positive attitude and be indifferent when he was ignored or diminished by people close to him. To stay positive and productive he probably had to repress his emotions of hate and rage along with his natural fierceness and capacity for aggression. To maintain his beneficial image of himself and his self-respect he probably became more controlled and rigid than he realized while appearing to be kind. Shaping himself in these ways would also limit his capacity to act in his own self-interest as well as to be creative, spontaneous, forceful, and even genuinely and actively caring for other people beyond his everyday encounters with them. Damn it all! I know all too well exactly what he did, and the cloud of illusions and denial he lived in.

As Dr. Jekyll's repressed characteristics began to coalesce and ferment under pressure over time, they began to make up what we call his dark shadow. Our shadow, like Dr. Jekyll's, becomes an alienated part of our personality, outside of our awareness, because we have shaped ourselves and been shaped by our environment to be indifferent to many of our strongest emotions, deepest needs, fiercest desires, and best potentials. Splitting ourselves this way curtails our ability to live with heart.

As Dr. Jekyll's repressed characteristics and alienated potentials accumulated, fermented, and turned destructive in his unconscious, they began to combine. When they progressed to a critical mass, they erupted and manifested themselves in the form of Mr. Hyde. When the pressure became too much, Mr. Hyde took over Dr. Jekyll's personality and behavior. He didn't know or care about being nice, fair, or politically correct. His awful acts are what I as a Jungian would call the eruption of the dark shadow, the uprising of one's inner deplorables. Everything that made up Mr. Hyde would threaten Dr. Jekyll's carefully constructed self-image. In using the term self-image I am not simply speaking of his persona—his public face that made him look successful, caring, and accomplished—I am speaking of the deeper self-image that gave him feelings of self-worth and made him think he was happy and satisfied in his life.

Dr. Jekyll, like most of us, probably came to admire in himself what was admired, respected, and valued by the people around him while he was growing up. In the same way, we create some kind of bubble of characteristics we value and take for granted. Our social group does the same thing, and as a social group we create a collective shadow as well.

## Grounds for Hope

Paradoxically, as I mentioned, some of our best potentials have frequently been blocked and shoved into our shadows. We call these aspects of our shadow our golden shadow. Some of our most important capacities for being courageous, creative, noble, outstanding, loving, and compassionate have gotten locked away in the unconscious compartments of our golden shadow. Even our most actively taught cultural ideals of achievement, success, productivity, and leadership are structured into social norms and not into individual depths, complexities, authenticities, and true higher callings.

For example, to be truly creative is to include the whole—the complexity and the truth of who we are. If we are open to change, if we realize that change is going to happen whether we like it or not, and if we understand that to some extent it is always a plunge into the unknown, our engagement will bring us to a better outcome. We soon learn that our tears and our rage can give us the energy to break out of the prison of our old models for living—the bondage of our old selves—and can activate and direct us toward other life-enhancing activities. They can give us the strength and courage to look a life change in the face and say, "Bring it on!"

William Blake, the passionate painter, poet, and visionary, summed up the interaction between the light and the dark symbolically by saying we should go to heaven for form and to hell for energy and then marry the two. We can use the emotional power (the power Dr. Jekyll repressed) from our rage, tears, and frustrations in our dark shadow to bring the potentials in our golden shadow to life. And they too will challenge our cultural norms and conventional wisdom.

In the next few chapters I will give you some

examples of how I, and our society, have created rage, despair, hopelessness, and attitudes of malignant aggression and how this energy should be moving us to change and realize potentials we have been indifferent to. This confrontation can lead to healing the divides within ourselves and within our culture. This confrontation can also lead us to visions of unity, the ability to direct our lives to vistas larger than ourselves, and to a new nobility of the spirit. The world ends in fire and ice in Norse mythology. Confronting ourselves, looking into the mirror of truth and breaking through the boundaries of our conventions and fears, is our journey into the ice and fire of new beginnings.

For a long time, I wondered why Mr. Hyde as Dr. Jekyll's shadow became so thoroughly evil and destructive. Slowly, through my life experiences, I have come to see that this is what alienation and dehumanization does to us, to anyone. Alienation on many levels causes rage and the urge—or the compulsion—to destroy life, social structures, and even one's self. Alienated individuals become trolls on the internet, and if they are cut off enough from themselves and society, they can become mass murderers and serial rapists. When alienated people come together, they become militia groups, cults, and terrorists. Alienated citizens can vote against their own self-interest out of rage and despair.

On a personal level, when we become alienated from our inner selves, our emotions, and our potentials that hold the power of our stagnated and unlived lives can drain our energy and leave us depressed, anxious, and vulnerable to illnesses and compulsive behaviors that can wreck our existence. The moment our shadow finally explodes is a dangerous one. But this moment can become the call to a whole new phase of life if we can learn to recognize and use the energy that is boiling up. This moment of potential healing and growth was lost to Dr. Jekyll due to his refusal to become self-aware, and it destroyed him. Throughout and since this election, we have experienced the eruption of the dark-shadow side of our social character. This moment too can be lost, can become more destructive if we refuse to search for the new awareness and understanding that it is demanding.

As I recognize, face, and integrate my capacities for rage, fierceness, aggression, or even a deep capacity to love—my own shadow qualities—I become stronger in knowing who I am. I have more resilience in dealing with life and more receptivity to love. (In reality, no matter what we think, very few of us are really receptive to love, especially self-love and self-compassion.) In addition, I gain the strength to be more vulnerable in showing passion and compassion and to take other personal risks. I also develop more capacity for experiencing a wide range of emotions and understanding what they are telling me about how I am living. The more of my shadow I can become aware of and integrate, the more vitality I will end up with, the more realistic my outlook on life will be, and my ability to understand others will grow in depth and breadth.

Confronting our shadows, as Dr. Jung articulates in his writings, is the most fundamental step in gaining any kind of spiritual or psychological maturity. To think this step can be avoided is to live in a state of illusion and denial. Neither education, will- power, enlightenment, positive thinking, endless counseling, prosperity, or simply belief-oriented religions can save us from needing to have the courage and insight to confront our shadows. Unfortunately, our culture gives us an implicit message that we should be active and in control of our lives. It also implies that being thoughtful and personally reflective is a waste of time. But we have to go through the ice and fire of seeking to genuinely know ourselves in order to heal the threats and bruises that cause our repressions in order to mine the gold within us to arrive at a fully satisfying life. This same principle holds true on a societal level. Confronting the shadow of our national character needs to become an ongoing event.

## Looking in the Mirror

For many of us, living in today's bubble of denial and illusion means being achievement-oriented, materially successful, well-fed and clothed, as safe as possible, and having lives that are moderately meaningful. There is also an undertow of fear in affluent people, especially those who are past midlife. Much of that fear is media-driven and causes us to fear people who are not like us, to fear losing our money and security, and to fear having things we value taken away from us. Deep inside of us we know, whether we can admit it to ourselves or not, that seismic shifts are needed in our society. We are afraid of what they may bring. But we need to remind ourselves that directly facing our problems, defining them, and seeking to understand their complexity is the first step in fostering a creative and beneficial outcome.

Thankfully our founding fathers and forebears were able to face their fears and reach beyond them to search for new horizons. However imperfect they were personally, they began the quest to create a society in which every citizen would be considered sacred.

From our bubble, our illusions of the "good life," our concerns for veterans, street people, poor mothers, malnourished children, the unemployed, the addicted, the mentally ill, and the sick have been given lip service and inadequate commitment. Too often we satisfy ourselves with giving a few dollars and small amounts of time to socially correct causes. Too easily we fall into the trap of denying the problems, blaming the victims or treating the symptoms and alleviating small amounts of pain. And, as much as I admire workers in those fields—as I once was—we, as a society, are not penetrating into the heart of darkness, the heart of our society's pain. Generally, too many of us leave it up to the government to help these groups, while too many of us in the top 20 percent of wage earners keep up a drumbeat of complaint about how ineffective the government is in administering these programs and how much they cost.

It is important to note that when Dr. Jekyll had worn out his specialized approach to the good life that had served him well up to this point, his vitality was usurped by his dark shadow—his sinister, repressed, violent side. Mr. Hyde represents the result of the parts of himself that Dr. Jekyll had been too nice and too focused on in his specialized approach to life (staying in his illusions of being a good person) to have the courage to try to understand the marginalized aspects of himself. We in the top 20 or 30 percent economically in our society have worn out our specialized approaches to living a genuinely prosperous life. It follows that some of the institutions supporting these approaches are also worn out. History has proven to us that social stagnation and accumulated frustration are far more dangerous than facing our fears and beginning the process of reimagining how we are structuring our present and future.

I can remember a lot about the path that took us up to 2016. I was there, and I saw that as the 1970s evolved into the 1980s, we as a country became more interested in productivity, achievement, materialism, enviable vocations, and appearing affluent. "Greed is good," and the creation of the illusion that it was good for all of us, was a major theme in the 1987 movie *Wall Street*. During the 1980s and 1990s, those of us in the bubble became more encapsulated in the focus on our personal well-being. Gradually we seemed to become indifferent to the increasing number of our fellow citizens who were becoming more insecure and even desperate, who were beginning to become angry and alienated. For too many of us it was too easy to label them "deplorables."

We must remember that the founding fathers of our country who wrote of the pursuit of happiness in our Declaration of Independence were products of the Enlightenment. They considered the pursuit of happiness as the enlargement of one's being through the development of the life of the mind and spirit.

Due in a large part to our national traumas during the 1960s and early 1970s, we seem to have lost faith in our government and our ability as citizens to affect it. We lost the personal commitment and personal obligation to be informed that are needed to ensure our government is of the people, by the people, and for the people. Such a government requires our full, informed engagement as citizens. Our indifference and frustration caused us to become subjects of the power-seeking ruling group and their agenda rather than free, responsible citizens. Frustrated subjects tend to revolt, while citizens act to create change.

I want to mention that here I am using the term deplorables as it was first used by the Democratic presidential candidate Hillary Clinton to describe the loud, angry, aggressive supporters of the other candidate, Donald Trump, in his rallies. She made the mistake of dehumanizing this group rather than seeking to understand their anger. This act cast them into the shadow of our national character and cut many of the rest of us off in our "respectable" bubbles. When we dehumanize a group, the question is not what side of politics we are on, but what side of humanity are we on. In the 2016 election both major parties spent plenty of time dehumanizing each other.

Our increasingly encapsulated approach to being politically involved has left the humanity, the hopes, and the dreams of many of our fellow citizens diminished and even demolished while we in our bubbles all too often project the cause of our societal problems onto these same people. The more these groups of people aren't listened to, the more they become part of our societal dark shadow. Just as with our personal dark-shadow characteristics, the more they become alienated from the mainstream in our society, the more bitter their anger and desperation becomes. As the story of Dr. Jekyll and Mr. Hyde approaches its climax, Dr. Jekyll cries out, "My devil has been long caged, he came out roaring." So has our collective shadow in the last few years. As Dr. Jung has noted, a person's feeling of weakness and non-existence eventually brings on the eruption of previously unknown desires for power.

When our societal shadow erupts (whether in riots, politics, mass murders, or exposed criminal activities in high places), we experience a time of fire and ice: Ragnorak—the Twilight of the Gods—symbolizing the end of some of the old dominant values and serious perspectives on how life should be lived that we have taken for granted. These are times that can scare us into a fearful retreat into an ultraconservative stance that is defensive, aggressive, spiritless, and heartless—a retreat out of our capacity to live with heart. Then hatred and ideologies seem to become zones of safety and comfort for those of us who choose these paths. The real call of destiny and of human nature that such times represent is a call to open ourselves to re-imagining who we are as a people, who we can become, and how we can live into a new unified national identity that has learned from what we have previously denied, repressed, and been indifferent to. This approach can help us become "stronger in our broken places," broader in our capacities to be human, and filled with new vitality.

When we think about our societal shadow, we need to remember that one of our great Western religions and wisdom traditions points out that before we judge someone else, we should examine ourselves (New Testament, Matthew 7:3-5 NIV). "Why do you look at the speck of sawdust in your brother's eye and pay no attention to the plank in your own eye?" In other words, before we judge someone or some situation we should look into our own shadow.

Knowing our own shadow is the prerequisite for perceiving our own reality and authenticity and is the beginning of being able to know the shadows of others and of our society. Dr. Jung says in his book *The Undiscovered Self* that a society is made up of individuals and that all real social change begins in the individual, especially when we are courageous enough to face our own shadow. Dr. Jung goes on to add that we in the Western world are beyond the point in history where a political figure or party can save us. We—you and I, individually—must take responsibility for our collective lives. Hoping to be saved by a candidate or party is stepping onto the path toward tyranny.

Because each one of us contributes to the structure of our collective personality and its shadow, we first must examine and understand our own illusions about life and how to live well. These illusions have been formed as we have grown up and developed. Our repressed and ignored shadows, our deplorables, must also be acknowledged in order to clearly understand what is going on in our collective personality. Far too many of our collective deplorables have been conditioned into lives of hopelessness, fear, anger, and mindsets—neural pathways of self-defeating aggressiveness, defensiveness, despair, withdrawal, and bitterness—while living in a world that is economically and politically indifferent to them. Understanding them begins with understanding ourselves. So, as I look at our political chaos more closely, I am going to start with facing myself.

The road to understanding myself and getting a true perspective on reality has required a difficult deprogramming of my indoctrination into thinking that I should have a positive attitude, appear happy, not burden others with my feelings, and be able to control and direct my life. It has taken courage to face these necessary changes in myself, and so does the humbling effort to continue to confront my shadow. It took courage to face the very discomforting fact that I have been wrong or negligent about a number of things rather than face the complex demands of being an active, responsible citizen. Over the years I have betrayed some of my deepest feelings, values, and potentials. It is also humbling that after eight decades of living I need to start over again to learn who I really am. If we can learn how to re-imagine ourselves based on the deeper truths of who we are, we will have a better foundation for re-imagining many areas in our government. In this way, we will be able to bring continuous renewal and vitality into our lives and culture.

# FIVE

# DARING TO BECOME VULNERABLE, AWARE, AND REALISTIC

*America's elite are worried that the country is falling behind China in mathematics, but they should start worrying that it is falling behind in a more fundamental way, in something that was considered America's strength: namely, the ability to stand up to any challenge, no matter how difficult or daunting.*

—*Azar Nafisi*

*The inner force, too, which, like the power of the atom, can either remake or shatter civilization, resides in the smallest unit of society, the individual.*

—*Sir Laurens Van Der Post*

Living forward, saying "bring it on!" to change, was a lesson I learned from a dream while I was living in denial of my life's true challenges. At the time, I woke up with a start, drenched with sweat. In the darkness of my dream, an enraged bear was chasing me through the crumbling gray stone walls of a burning castle. My interpretation: the solid structures of my old life were being destroyed, and this great fierce beast from my shadow wanted to devour the old me.

New life, fierceness, and vitality come from our own confrontations with our shadows. These shadows are energies and realities in our lives that we have denied and repressed. When I put myself in a bubble of illusion, or a skewed view of life, and cut myself off from the struggle with what I think are my darker energies and realities, I rob myself of the dynamic, internal conflicts that are needed for my growth, for my quest for wholeness, and for the fulfillment of the inner dream of my potentials. These struggles give me the energetic life force that can ripple out into the world in a beneficial way. And make no mistake about this fact. The things we hide, cover up, and deny within ourselves also ripple out and contribute to the negativity around us and in the world. The first question I had to ask myself was how I got into this isolated, one-sided bubble to begin with.

Barbara Ehrenreich, the well-known author and social commentator, explains one of the key factors that helps reinforce the walls of our bubbles in her very important book *Bright-Sided: How the Relentless Promotion of Positive Thinking Has Undermined America*. Please read this book—I will mention here a few points that affected me and contributed to maintaining my bubble, but I don't have the space to fully explain this disaster in our society. Barbara forcefully explains how positive thinking has become an ideology, an unconscious creed, an almost religious dogma that gets structured into most of us as we develop and is always in the background of how we perceive other people and situations. We are taught that having or expressing any kind of negative thought is an unacceptable, unhealthy way of life rather than just a point of view or a realistic reaction to circumstances. This ideology, she states, "encourages us to deny reality, submit cheerfully to misfortune, and blame only ourselves for our fate."

It infuriates me to realize she is right. Positive thinking, as we experience it, causes us to become delusional, urging us to see the glass as half full when it actually lies shattered on the floor. We are subjects to the tyranny of positive thinking.

When I have said to various people that I don't believe in positive thinking, they often respond by saying, "Do you think I'm better off by being negative?" or "What good is being negative?" or "What purpose does getting angry serve?" The answers are simple. What is best for us is to let ourselves experience our honest emotional responses to the situations in our lives. These kinds of responses make us real, keep us engaged in life, and make us better able to deal with the reality we are facing.

Barbara Ehrenreich goes on to say:

> In addition, positive thinking has made itself useful as an apology for the crueler aspects of the market economy. If optimism is the key to material success, and if you can achieve an optimistic outlook through the discipline of positive thinking, then there is no excuse for failure. The flip side of positivity is thus a harsh insistence on personal responsibility: if your business fails or your job is eliminated, it must be because you didn't try hard enough, didn't believe firmly enough in the inevitability of your success. As the economy has brought more layoffs and financial turbulence to the middle

class, the promoters of positive thinking have increasingly emphasized this negative judgment: to be disappointed, resentful, or downcast is to be a "victim" and a "whiner".

I might add to these statements that a number of people take this same position about our physical and mental health.

For decades I thought that whenever I met or talked with anyone—be it family, friends, colleagues, or strangers—I should give the appearance of being positive, happy, and moving toward successful achievements and should present all of my family members in the same light. After all, America's official belief for decades (for people in my bubble class) was that things are good and getting better. Part of the shock of the economic crash of 2008 and the election of 2016 has been the direct confrontation between that belief system for people in the bubble and the reality of everyone else. Since the election, it has been much harder to hold on to the habit of positive thinking. Awakening from nightmares can shatter our delusions.

As I reflected on how I became more entrenched in my bubble, I realized that I had been working so hard on my vocation, my writing, and my family concerns that I had denied many of my deepest feelings and fears. I had also forgotten that what happens to one of us in our society also affects all of us and the climate of the culture we live in. I had also banished many of my strongest social concerns into a twilight zone where I was only semiconscious of them. In fact, the circumstances of my life and spirit had been deeply hurt by our economic disaster in 2008 and the collapse of our mental health systems, the harshness and greed of our medical insurance systems, the student debt in my family, and the lack of job security for the generations in my family following me.

If we deny or fail to accept the seriousness of our outrage, frustration, bitterness, and fear long enough in general or particular areas (in my case, those broader social concerns that actually affected me deeply) we can soon seem to forget we have these feelings and not know how to articulate them. But, as Dr. Jekyll discovered, when we close our eyes and ears to our feelings, whether they are within ourselves or within our collective social character, they don't go away. They fester inside. Keeping them repressed requires more energy, and that causes increasing unconscious stress. Then we only know that we feel sluggish, depressed, and out of sorts, or we have problems with our spouses and children, or we have problems with our weight, or we eat or drink or even exercise too much.

One of our best defenses against facing our reality is to scapegoat some part of ourselves, some perceived weakness, such as a weakness for food, sex, alcohol, reading mysteries, and so forth. Then we can get into an emotional gridlock of struggling with ourselves over our lack of self-control and avoid facing our real reality altogether. In reality, our social character—our collective "we"—follows a similar pattern.

The bone-deep brainwashing into positive thinking that I was subject to growing up has kept me from looking at the bigger picture of different people's circumstances in our society. It has also kept me from fully seeking to understand the nature of their experiences and their lives and how our blindness is affecting them. I have many concerns about our society, and I'm sure you have your own. But my indoctrination particularly limited my perspective on reality in the following five areas: (1) the American dream, (2) people in poverty, (3) health care, (4) mental health care, and (5) the economic crash of 2008. As I discuss each area, I will explain the bubble I was in, give voice to my dark shadow—the honest feelings I repressed—give voice to my golden shadow, which gives hope, and describe some of my ideas as to how I would like to see these challenges met.

# PART III

## Confronting Our Pain
## and Growing Beyond It

*To understand is not to permit. But to fail to understand is
the surest guarantee of a mounting strife which will assault
the well-being of every citizen. And therefore ... the first task
before us is this: an effort to understand.*

—Robert F. Kennedy

*Happiness lies not in the mere possession of money; it
lies in the joy of achievement, in the thrill of creative
effort. The joy and moral stimulation of work no longer
must be forgotten in the mad chase of evanescent profits.
These dark days will be worth all they cost us if they teach
us that our true destiny is not to be ministered unto but to
minister to ourselves and to our fellow men.*

—Franklin Delano Roosevelt

# SIX

# ISN'T IT TIME TO FACE THE HEART OF DARKNESS BENEATH OUR FAÇADE OF AFFLUENCE?

*Our humanity is our burden, our life. We need not battle for it; we need only do what is infinitely more difficult—that is, accept it.*

*—James Baldwin*

I am staggered to realize that we have lost a central pillar in the American dream. On the surface I would say that this loss means too many of us have lost our confidence in our ability to earn a steady, respectable living. But down deep in the tribal soul of my cultural unconscious, I know that I need to feel like I am valuable because I am working at something that contributes to the world I live in. And so do most people. Shortly before his assassination, Martin Luther King Jr. assured the garbage workers in Memphis, Tennessee, that they had dignity because they worked, were self-responsible, and made a contribution to society.

*That our lives make a difference*

We all need to feel competent at what we are doing, that we are building and living lives that are valued, and that we are part of a community, connected to other people. These factors are major contributors to a satisfying life. They also shelter the promise that we can earn a better life and that we and our children can thrive in society. Without the above possibilities, we begin to lose our sense of self-worth, dignity, and belonging to our society—and we lose faith in ourselves as worthy human beings.

Powerful forces of change, innovation, and greed have swept over our world while we in the illusion that things are or will be getting better have been politically asleep at the wheel. When I look back on the business my partner and I founded, which I left over four decades ago to pursue a new vocation, I remember it as a business I loved. Developing it had been a risky, exciting adventure, and it provided employment and needed goods to people at affordable prices. I am still proud of this period in my life. But only recently have I become deeply disturbed to realize that due to many of our plants and mills moving out of this country my business would have disappeared out from under me within a few years if I had stayed in it. My overfocus on my future and my preoccupation with the illnesses in my family contributed to my losing sight of the forces taking over a part of the world I cared a great deal about. I was also blind as to how these forces were violating some of my deepest values.

In the shadow-land of my soul, I have known, as have most of us, that industries have been shutting down and moving overseas for decades. Merciless downsizing and restructuring have become common. These are economic earthquakes that have generated hard consequences as people have experienced the American dream turning into a nightmare. In these devastating situations, people lose their jobs, identities, communities, and security. Moreover, people who keep their jobs face decreasing pensions and health insurance benefits. All too often they are also left with the fear they will be next. Furthermore, more and more workers, including highly skilled ones, are becoming contract employees. They generally have few to no employee benefits or job security. Our workforce today, including many professionals and academics, lives in an ongoing climate of fear—and this group also contains my children and their families.

From factory and service workers to upper-management people, jobs are threatened and insecure, which means one's whole way of life feels like it is built on sand. In other words, one's identity, source of meaning, purpose and community has no secure foundation. As a consequence, the towns supporting many of today's industries and businesses can become impoverished overnight if and when the businesses pull out. It is not hard to understand why people in all of the above circumstances can vote in anger, seemingly against their own best interests, when in reality they are voting against a government and a field of politicians, both of which they feel have betrayed them and have no interest in their well-being. It is little wonder that many people are filled with rage covering their fear and despair. There is a chamber in the cells of my shadow where I agree with them.

Recently I watched Oliver Stone's 1987 movie *Wall Street* for the first time in years. The movie reminded me of the greed and ruthlessness that can and often does possess venture capitalism. The movie does a dramatic job of showing how players in this game pitch what they are doing as being good for everyone. The movie ends with Bud, the young man who emulated the big-time player Gordon Gekko, having a change of conscience, turning state's evidence, going to prison, and regaining the value and satisfaction of a clear conscience. Unfortunately, my conscience is not so clear because I have remained an indifferent citizen as this approach to business developed and became firmly rooted in our culture at the expense of many good people.

I watched *Wall Street* because a friend had told me how upset he was at what the venture capitalists were doing with the company he had founded and that they had purchased from him. At the same time, I was reading the book *Bill Moyers Journal: The Conversation Continues*. When I flipped over to his interview with Barbara Ehrenreich, the author and social commentator, I was knocked to my knees by Bill Moyers' opening statement.  Here I quote several paragraphs directly from his book:

> When the predators of high finance spot their prey, they can move with terrible swiftness. In 2007, *Wall Street Journal* reporter Ianthe Jeanne Dugan described how the private equity firm Blackstone Group swooped down on a travel reservation company in Colorado, bought it, laid off 841 employees, and recouped their entire investment in just seven months, one of the quickest returns on capital ever for such a deal.

> Blackstone made a killing while ordinary workers were left to sift through the debris of their devastated lives. They sold their homes to make ends meet, lost their health insurance, took part-time jobs making sandwiches and coffee.

That fall, Blackstone's chief executive, Stephen Schwarzman, reportedly worth billions of dollars, rented a luxurious resort in Montego Bay, Jamaica, to celebrate the marriage of his son. The bill reportedly came to $50,000, plus thousands more to sleep 130 guests. Add to that drinks on the beach, dancers and a steel band, marshmallows around the fire, and the following day an opulent wedding banquet with champagne, jazz band, and a fireworks display that alone cost $12,500. Earlier in the year Schwarzman had rented out the Park Avenue Armory in New York (his thirty-five-room apartment couldn't hold the five hundred guests) to celebrate his sixtieth birthday. Cost: $3 million.

So? It's his money, isn't it? Yes, but consider this: the stratospheric income of private-equity partners is taxed at only 15 percent. That's less than the rate paid by the struggling middle class. When Congress considered raising the rate paid on their Midas-like compensation, these financial titans sent their lobbyist mercenaries swarming over Washington and brought the "debate" to an end in less time than it had taken Schwarzman to fire 841 workers.

Our ruling class had won another round in a fight that Barbara Ehrenreich has been documenting for years. After studying theoretical physics at Reed College and earning a doctorate from Rockefeller University, Ehrenreich joined a small nonprofit in the late 1960s, advocating for better health care for the poor. She began researching and writing investigative stories for the organization's monthly bulletin and went on to journalistic prominence with articles and essays for *Ms.*,

*Mother Jones, The Atlantic Monthly,* and *Harper's Magazine,* among others.

Ehrenreich reports on inequality in America by stepping into the real-life shoes of the people who experience it. For her bestselling book *Nickel and Dimed: On (Not) Getting By in America,* she worked as a waitress, cleaning woman, and a Walmart sales clerk, testing what it's like to live on $7 an hour. (Damned near impossible.) She went undercover again, looking for a white-collar job and writing about it in *Bait and Switch: The (Futile) Pursuit of the American Dream.* She saw so many professional people falling to the bottom rung of jobs that she launched an organization— United Professionals—to fight back against the war on the middle class "that is undermining so many lives."

After reading Moyer's article and talking to other people I thought, "My God, what are we coming to? Have we as a country lost our minds, our conscience, or both? No wonder the anger beneath the surface of our civility is breaking out in crime, violence, addiction, and reckless voting. Have I lost my conscience? No, I've had my head in the sand and by my indifference I have contributed to the evil in our landscape. I am a capitalist. I worked for a major corporation early in my life, started my own business, and still have my own practice. Though capitalism isn't perfect I think it is the best economic system in the world and can offer the most opportunities to the most people. But when it loses its heart, and money and power become more important to its leaders than the good of our country and its people, then it has a devastating dark side.

Rebecca Solnit, another well-known writer and

social commentator, compares capitalism as a creator of ongoing disasters to a child that hasn't been potty-trained. We are left to clean them up like a frustrated mother or, to extend her analogy, to try to discipline the child to clean up after itself through legislation or protests. As much as I like this analogy and admire Ms. Solnit, I think she is understating the case. The dark side of capitalism is becoming more like a cholera epidemic that is calling for us to put a government in place that can continuously clean up and control an economic system that should be here to serve us and not to hold us hostage. At this point, with my head fully out of the sand, I have to ask:

- Wouldn't it be better if we recognized that in today's complex world of communications, multinational corporations, and a very heterogeneous population, Americans don't need to be entertaining the notion of less government? We need to focus strength, energy, and determination on creating good government.

- Wouldn't it be better to recognize that in the era of giant corporations a so-called "free market" is impossible? A government for the people is needed to insure people are more important than profits, especially short-term ones.

- Wouldn't it be better to recognize that the political stances supporting "free markets" are serving corporations and not we, the people— no matter how these corporations and their politicians pitch it?

- Wouldn't it be better if we remembered that we do have power? Communication, protesting, and voting are power!

- Wouldn't it be better if our government steered value-driven capitalistic forces toward combating climate change?

- And wouldn't it be better if we remembered that the forces that want to undermine a government of the people, by the people, and for the people thrive on us believing that we don't have enough power, that we can't make a difference, so there is no reason to act?

Working together we can damn well change it all for the better.

\* \* \* \*

Forty thousand people lost their jobs in the late 1960s when the elevators in Chicago were automated. I was shocked to hear the brutal results of this step forward in "progress." I heard these numbers from the conservative commentator William F. Buckley, on his TV show Firing Line. He then asked the question, "What are we going to do about that?" Since then, while automation and robotics have continued to replace humans, the answer is essentially, "Nothing!" Manufacturing, service industries, banking, retailing—you name it—are being swept by these trends. In our passivity, we have become desensitized and look at the people affected as numbers, statistics, and not as real human beings. But they are human beings, and they may be you. Experts predict that over 50 percent of future jobs are at risk. If not you, then surely your children, grandchildren, and their families will be dramatically affected. Stop and think about what it would mean to lose your financial security, your dignity, your identity, and your place in your community. We had better wake up fast or we are going to be creating hopeless, angry people by the tens of thousands.

In this case, other industrialized nations are doing a far better job of looking out for the dignity and well-being of their citizens than we are. And, once again, I must admit that I am ashamed of myself. This situation and the others I have written about remind me of the statement made by the twentieth-century theologian and ethicist Reinhold Niebuhr. He said, "Most evil is not done by evil people but by good people who don't know what they are doing."

Niebuhr is referring to "good people" who refuse to open their eyes and do not want to see. They do not want to unplug their ears and they do not want to listen. They do not want to have their thoughts ignited, and they do not want to think. Most of all they do not want to confront their shadows and society's shadows because looking at themselves would disturb their illusions about themselves, that they are "good people" who are aware of and thinking about important things.

When I participate as a citizen in creating or allowing an economic system to diminish people and deny them the essentials of life's necessities that would give them a chance, through hard work and devotion, to fulfill the promise of their sacred lives, then I am participating in creating a climate of evil. And make no mistake about it, the results of unmanaged change that can leave people feeling impotent, alienated, apathetic, and hopeless becomes the breeding ground for violence, addiction, and abusive relationships. suicide

Greed & Power - love is absent - empathy is absent.

## Daring to Wake Up

Nothing can be changed until it is recognized, fully faced, and accepted. We all need to look in the mirror and see how cold and heartless we have become in ignoring the well-being of our neighbors, our fellow countrymen, women, and, God forbid, our children. Once again, every other major industrialized nation has done a better job of providing safety nets and transition paths and respecting the dignity of its citizens than we have.

I am ashamed that our country is nowhere near being number one in taking care of our citizens—of each other. I am ashamed of my blindness and my silence as a citizen, my denial of what should have outraged me, and my failure to own my responsibility. I am afraid that I wanted our politicians to do a good job of running the country without bothering me. I should have known that is not democracy.

We who have been in our bubbles of denial and illusion need to be awakened to our repressed anger, like the bear in my dream, to give us the strength and determination to open our eyes and transform our government back into one that is of the people, by the people, and for the people. Outrage, struggle, and hope call for courage and action, and we must renew the soul and promise of America now and for the future.

The great statement by Abraham Lincoln in his Gettysburg Address on a blood-soaked battleground to a divided nation shows us that the true American spirit can find its highest values in our darkest times. In my mind, his words break down in the following way:

- "Of the people" means making a continuous effort to pursue our highest values and potentials.
- "By the people" means we must be fully engaged with our government as citizens who are doing

their best to be informed, mature, and self-responsible.

- "For the people" means being sure that our government is striving to support the well-being of every citizen.

My deepest values tell me that if I am indifferent to the people whose way of life, security, and dignity are being threatened, I am diminishing their humanity and robbing myself of my own. I have to ask, wouldn't it be better if we created a government that helped manage these changes, that gave our citizens a safety net, and that supported their ability to feel secure in a lifetime that in the future might have numerous job changes? Wouldn't it be better if we realized that doing these things was also the most economically sound path for our country in the long run?

SEVEN

·─────·◆·─────·

# POOR AND HOPELESS
# IN THE LAND OF PLENTY

*The curse of poverty has no justification in our age. It is socially as cruel and blind as the practice of cannibalism at the dawn of civilization when men ate each other because they had not yet learned to take food from soil or to consume the abundant animal life around them. The time has come for us to civilize ourselves by the total, direct, and immediate abolition of poverty.*
*—Martin Luther King, Jr.*

Writing this book has caused me to peel back the layers in my memory of other times of crises. I was thirty-two years old when my hometown, Atlanta, Georgia, was in deep shock. It was late 1969. The city was reeling... brutalized after the assassinations of President Kennedy, Martin Luther King, Jr., and Robert Kennedy. The city was blanketed with rage and grief, scared and shaken to its foundations by the news and images of riots, burning cities, and antiwar protests. A silent scream arose from the downtown Tenth Street area where the bodies of drugged-out teenagers and hippies littered the streets like corpses. A dark cloud of disbelief, bitterness, and despair permeated the city's atmosphere.

My blood ran cold as I, a young family man, watched the foundations of our world crumble. "Good God! What kind of future have I brought my children into?" I wondered. Driven by an ambition to give my family a good life and to make my mark in the world, I had, at a young age, become a senior executive in the famed department store, Rich's. Rich's was a premier business in the city of Atlanta and, after the federal and state governments, the largest employer in Georgia. Looking for an additional way to make a difference in our community, I discovered that Rich's had a program that paid tuition for executives to continue their graduate education. Since I was already past the point in my career when an MBA would be of benefit, I enrolled in a new master's program at Georgia State University in what was then termed "urban life." This program was contemporary and focused on the problems our cities were facing; in addition, GSU was and is a large, dynamic city college in the heart of downtown Atlanta.

While attending night classes, I learned about the Central Presbyterian Church's inner-city clinics. Located downtown, across from the state capitol building, the clinics centered around a baby clinic, which was treating almost 6,000 babies a year. The clinic included a pharmacy, a dental clinic, a family planning clinic, a pastoral counseling center, a drug treatment center, an afterschool childcare center, a surplus-food distribution program, and a cafeteria that was open daily. These clinics were supported financially by the church and with volunteers, with no active evangelizing allowed in them at all.

Galvanized by the spirit of what they were doing, I wanted to get to work helping my city face its problems. The motivating force behind these clinics was the kind of community spirit I wanted for my family. We joined that church, even though I had been out of organized religion for years, and I became a volunteer in the clinics for almost a decade. My first day as a volunteer-in-training was as a counselor in the methadone treatment center. When I walked through the door, it was as if a bullet had struck me. My heart stopped...and when it began to pound again, I felt like I had been flung into a scene from Dante's Inferno. The patients were like ghosts. Young wraiths  looking like they had just been released from a concentration camp. Guards stood with hands on their guns to keep anyone from trying to grab them. "Holy shit! Is this America?" I thought.

I had chosen to work in this clinic because I was full of rage and despair at the number of teenagers, mostly runaways and most of them from decent families, who were lying in drug-induced stupors on our downtown streets, being victimized by constant violence and unspeakable brutality. I saw a vision of hell that I had never dreamed was possible in this country, in my town. I eventually became the chairman of the clinics and served in several different areas. Meanwhile, my mainstream life was evolving as well. After a couple of years, I left Rich's, and a partner and I started our own group of stores. Circumstances later took me back to graduate school in counseling psychology at Georgia State University. Georgia State was two blocks from the clinics where I continued to volunteer.

Clinic work took me straight into the heart of the

housing projects in Atlanta, with its primarily black population, while delivering surplus food. This was my first face-to-face encounter with inner-city poverty. I had known rural poverty—black and white—growing up, but this inner-city experience was totally new to me, strange and scary. As a boy in grammar school, my family had lived in the country outside of Atlanta. While we were not poor, many of the people around us were. In my fifth-grade classroom, at least 20 percent of the students were in their teens, just sitting at their desks, as required by law, doing nothing but waiting to turn sixteen so they could drop out of school and go to work. Needless to say, with so many frustrated older kids around, there was plenty of bullying directed toward us younger kids. This was the year I learned to live with my inner alarm system on, all the time. By the time I was in the sixth grade, I was carrying a switchblade for self-defense. Fortunately, because I was big for my age, I never had to use it.

But years later, the first time I stepped into a building in the housing projects, I felt I had been dropped into a well so deep that everything was unsure, paralyzing, and frightening—different from the poverty that I had known. Quickly, I began to understand how Robert F. Kennedy's exposure to poor people in Bedford-Stuyvesant and their desperate sadness caused him to question the truths he had taken for granted, softened him, opened his heart, and began the true maturation of his character. His character became, as I hope mine has, one that wasn't bound by the silly, defensive definitions of progressive, liberal, or conservative, but one that was strong and compassionate.

So much of what I encountered in every apartment, in every courtyard, was heart-wrenching. Once I became known in the area—it took months—I found that many of the people were warm, especially the older folks who often had a wry sense of humor in spite of their conditions. However, even though I got to know them well, it didn't mean I really understood them. I hadn't walked in their shoes. But when we drove our van into the area, I could sense the feelings of impotence and anger bubbling beneath the surface, and aggression was always close to the boiling point in the young men. All too often, the victims of their angst were each other.

It doesn't take much imagination to see that these young men and women, stuck in their societal impotence, would turn in dark directions out of these frustrations. I wasn't surprised to see them turn to drugs to escape. Nor was I surprised to see them take the dark path by joining a gang to gain a sense of dignity, identity, meaning and purpose

Violence feeds on feelings of powerlessness, hopelessness, and blindness to the possibilities of a better life in the future. This is not to say that many of these people did not work. They did, but in low-paying, grinding jobs that had no dignity in the eyes of our materialistic society. People in the more affluent bubble seem to have a hard time imagining you can work hard—two or three jobs—work harder than you ever believed possible and still sink deeper into the abyss of debt, poverty, hopelessness, homelessness, and rage. The inhabitants of this world focus on daily survival, not on building a better life.

After almost a decade of volunteer work with the clinics I had to leave, due to illness in my family. But the desperate sense of sadness I had felt in it seared my heart and left it with a silent cry and bitter tears tucked in a deep corner. Holy Mother of God! We should have

been doing better than this a long time ago. And any
s.o.b. who thinks these people are just lazy, indolent,
and milking the system while living off the rest of us
should try walking in their shoes for a few months.

* * * *

As I look back and mentally travel my road again,
more truth emerges from those times in my life. Certain
truths, which because of its pain and the blur of how
overwhelming my life had become due to my wife's
illness, got pushed into my unconscious—my shadow.
That shadow became a lockbox for my anger and
despair.Memories from that era in my life are stuck in
the recesses of my mind like snapshots in an old photo
album that my soul won't let me discard. Sometimes they
just pop into my vision like someone had just pressed the
button on a PowerPoint presentation. At this moment,
I'll share one just to give you a flavor of what I can't
forget.

I see myself in a room with twelve master's-level
students in counseling whom I am supervising during
their practicum. I am a doctoral student and they are
all working in inner-city facilities close to mine. A thir-
ty-two-year-old African American woman is presenting
a case she is trying to handle. It is that of a thirteen-
year-old girl who had been raped in the tenements and
had become pregnant. (God only knows how the baby
was delivered.) The police had been called when she was
caught stealing milk from a convenience store to feed
her baby. The police went back with her to get her baby
at the abandoned building where she was living. As the
student presented this case, tears rolled down her cheeks.
The brave little girl my student was trying to help was
doing all she could to try to take care of her baby, whom

she had diapered with newspapers. This snapshot still haunts me over four decades later because I know the society that I am a so-called responsible member of has done far too little about these darkest expressions of our irresponsibility and lack of seriousness.

This tiny African American girl loved her baby dearly and knew it loved her. By this time, in the classroom, tears were in all our eyes. We knew the system and we knew this little girl and her baby would be torn apart. The student counselor was doing all she could to get good placements for them. We knew their lives could not continue in any safe sense in an abandoned building, and yet they were going to lose the only love either one of them had ever known. What could I say as the supervisor to teach or heal or whatever in this situation? Once again, once again, in this wasteland of a world, I felt my helplessness. And I felt rage and shame at the pain our culture is blind to…at the lack of compassion in a rich society that squanders so much of its humanity in useless, wasteful ways. Why is it so hard for us to see the deep pain, suffering, rage, and hopelessness right down the street from us?

*    *    *    *

When I left this inner-city work, I felt as if I and my fellow workers were like the little Dutch boy in the Hans Christian Andersen story "The Silver Skates." You may remember the little Dutch boy from your childhood. He saw water seeping through a small hole in a dike that was holding back the sea in an isolated part of town. He stuck his finger in the hole to stop the flow because if it had continued, the hole would have grown larger from the force of the water until the dike would have burst and destroyed the town. He stayed there bravely throughout the freezing night, hoping for help. Finally, in the morning, the grown-ups awakened, found him, and rescued the town. We were like him, except most of the grown-ups are still having trouble waking up, even now, forty years later. Poverty still affects one in seven of all Americans. An amazing number of our children are hungry, sick, and unable to focus in school. Plus, for over three decades economic inequality has expanded to the point where the ever-widening gap between the wealthy and the poor is now considered to be the most destructive social problem we are facing.

\* \* \* \*

Take it from someone who has known our world rather well. The theologian Reinhold Niebuhr is exactly right. If we don't really know consciously and with full awareness who we are and what we are doing, we are going to end up doing evil in spite of our best intentions. Fast-forward forty-plus years. We know more today than we did when I was working in the inner city. What we now know has validated many of the intuitions and answered some of the questions I had about how, after sometimes only a generation, the poor are trapped in their circumstances, and why, without knowing it, they continue to self-destruct through violence and addictions, failing to come to grips with their lives in a helpful, hopeful way. Of course, this reality says something about the indifference of the rest of us as well.

J. D. Vance in his memoir *Hillbilly Elegy* tells how his mother, who had overcome obstacles to become a trained nurse, failed to make it out of the entangled clutches of the culture of the Appalachian poor she grew up in. Her life was a howl of hope and pain. Every time she seemed to break free, she fell back into the swamp of addictions, destructive relationships, and conflicts that sucked her down once again. Similar things happen to poor people everywhere, whether they are in Appalachia or the inner city or any other area where they are consistently living in impoverished surroundings.

Over forty years ago, I realized that it didn't take a psychoanalyst or a scientist to see that there was a mindset or a mental template of some kind that developed in the majority of people living in impoverished surroundings, especially in the second and third generations. Studies in neuroscience today point out that kids growing up in poverty have smaller brains than normal and that this results in a decreased ability to make good judgments and a low capacity for ethical processing. Impoverished children have a loss of brain tissue in areas that support making decisions, solving problems, controlling emotional behavior, following instructions, and paying attention. We have also learned, however, that the brain has neuroplasticity—the capacity to modify its own structure—and that we never completely outgrow this wonderful potential. That is why, with the proper training while in the Marine Corps, J. D. Vance was able to turn his own "learned helplessness" into "learned willfulness."

## Learned Helplessness—What Really Scares Me

Learned helplessness in poverty circumstances is a state in which people have been indoctrinated into the belief that the choices they make have little or no effect on improving their lives and that they have no control over their circumstances. These mindsets are not attitudes that can be easily changed at will or by having an insightful moment. They are patterned into one's brain. Changing these patterns requires a structured learning program like the one J. D. Vance encountered in the Marine Corps, where he was retrained and taught, in his words, "learned willfulness."

It looks to me like the black poor, white poor, city poor, country poor, Appalachian poor, and other poor people share a similar mindset of learned helplessness, especially after more than one generation of poverty. These people find it almost impossible to genuinely imagine having a better life or, if they can, how to get there. They cannot really see themselves in a life that would provide a reasonable degree of safety, a good steady job, and a step up into the middle class. To move up to a better lifestyle is to move into a new community and a new social group which has a set of norms, values, perceptions, and activities the poor know as little about as people born into affluence know about what it is really like to be poor.

And here is another point. Moving up can even increase someone's anger and bitterness. Just imagine what it might be like to move into a world where the complexities of banking, tax forms, traversing the insurance markets, effectively buying a house and car, interviewing for a job, and many other things are confusing, belittling, and enraging. It would be like being dropped into another country, where all the known customs, laws, and coping skills no longer work.

While in a certain sense we have some helpful programs targeting poor people, they are generally not aimed at giving them a genuine, realistic hand-up. J. D. Vance was fortunate: he is very intelligent, had a helpful grandmother, and found a hand to help him up in the Marines. We also face another problem because we have such an adverse political attitude toward taxes for people who can afford to pay them that we parse out assistance to the poor based on income levels. This bias causes many problems, such as poor mothers having to choose between paid work, childcare, and sometimes medical care or food. It also slams people on the income borderlines who are slipping backward and members of the middle class who are sinking for the third time.

Here is what really scares me. We are creating a daily-growing group living in semi-poverty. They serve in restaurants, care for the very young and the elderly, work in distribution centers and stores as salesclerks and stockers, and so on. Plenty of them are educated yet seem stuck. The server in one of our favorite restaurants has a degree in architecture. The middle-aged fellow who cheerfully greets me almost daily in Starbucks is a former high school teacher with a master's degree. He moved here to care for ailing parents and can't find a teaching job. Think about this reality. Could this soon be one of your children, or your grandchildren, or your spouse or partner, or you? How fast are we creating, on an even larger scale, the circumstances J. D. Vance grew up in? These people are human beings just like us who have needs and fears and want to have hopes and dreams for themselves and their families. Can those of us who resent paying taxes learn that we help ourselves when we help others recognize and fulfill their sacred potentials?

Americans have the resources and the knowledge to do better than we are; as we fail to give a hand to people struggling in the above situations, they become angry or apathetic voters because they feel excluded from being valued by the rest of us and assume, rightfully so, that our government has no interest in their well-being. The answer to these problems is modest, in that it involves common sense, and is challenging, in that implementing common sense isn't as easy as you might think. Of course, we must stop kicking people while they are down, which means stop underpaying people for the work they do. We must also respect their dignity -- these people are adding value to our country by working. Then the solutions I'm suggesting in the next chapter are not radical. They are simply common sense.

# EIGHT

# DARING TO WAKE UP: PURPOSE-DRIVEN HELP WHERE IT IS NEEDED

> *You cannot build character and courage by taking away people's initiative and independence. You cannot help people permanently by doing for them what they could and should do for themselves.*
>
> —*Abraham Lincoln*

*love's service*

There was a revolutionary called Jesus who taught us the value in our lives of love, justice, healing the sick, and helping the poor. We are worse off because out of our fear we stubbornly do not live what he came to teach us. We need to learn how to be helpful to the poor and to each other. Pity frequently isn't helpful, and compassion may not be much better. Handouts are necessary in the case of the absolutely helpless, but they should be given so that a very sick, aged, or disabled person can live in dignity. We must give from our concern for a suffering fellow human being. Being

*compassion is a verb!*

judgmental is of no value. Condemning the poor, the semi-poor, and others of us who are struggling with personal failures or failing at being individually responsible is arrogantly defensive on our part and may be a purposeful misunderstanding of the entire situation. A helping hand and the realization that we are all part of the human family and citizens of a country that considers every person sacred are what is needed now.

Isn't it time that we remember and learn from our own history? Didn't President Franklin Roosevelt give a helping hand—not a hand-out mind you—to the largest number of people in our history in the New Deal? His programs taught to men and women, who were sinking for the third time, character structure, life skills, job skills, how to see themselves working in the future, and how to live in a new level of society that many of them had never been exposed to.

In today's world we need to re-focus on living with an attitude that reflects caring, purpose, self-respect, meaning, and valuing each other. We also need to regain the value of working together for our common good. The New Deal programs taught people the value of community and of service to it.

In the atmosphere of today's world, it seems increasingly hard to teach the values that make our lives worth living; such values as seeing our work as meaningful, our relationships as treasures, our families as potential for fulfillment rather than as mere obligation, our educational systems as sources of a rich life, and our homes as a place to rest our heads. We need to return our government's focus to supporting the values that make life worthwhile, to be of the people, by the people, and for the people.

We are led to a better way when we remember that

character structure, work ethics, healthy ambition, and civility are values and skills that must be learned. And if they must be learned, we must be able to also teach them. (U.S. Senator Ben Sasse has a lot to add to this topic in his book *The Vanishing American Adult: Our Coming-of-Age Crisis—and How to Rebuild a Culture of Self-Reliance.*)

The grounded New Deal approach provided adults, young and older, a practical, mature entrance into a new life of meaning and satisfaction in contrast to our current greater culture's fantasy of achieving fame and super-earnings while fulfilling one's potential or dreams. Young adults and older ones who have the foundation of their lives shaken or never formed need a hand up. Believe me, I know; I've been there. Finding my own version of the New Deal approach after finishing college, in a way that did nothing to help me into adulthood, created a foundation for my life that enabled me to live creatively while also facing many hardships and challenges over the years.                          *build resilience*

The New Deal programs opened their participants' eyes to a broader vision of life, they approached them as the Marines approached J. D. Vance. In both cases, they engaged participants and recruits as if they knew nothing in terms of life skills. Both programs realized the students needed to unlearn weak attitudes and habits. And as they taught them how to have a new vision of themselves in life, they also taught them how to pursue this vision through action, purpose, self-discipline, and commitment.

In the New Deal, the Civilian Conservation Corps (CCC) provided work and purpose to more than three million young men before it was over. The CCC was devoted to reclaiming our forest lands and our environment. Reserve army officers were called back into service to oversee the project. The well-known historian Doris Kearns Goodwin, in her book *Leadership in Turbulent Times*, gives a moving and dramatic history of the New Deal in chapter eleven, "Turnaround Leadership, Franklin Roosevelt and the Hundred Days." I hope you and every candidate for office will read this book.

The Public Works Administration was meant to encourage private enterprise to build immense projects to benefit our society and that would endure. The author above lists the Bonneville Dam, the Lincoln Tunnel, La Guardia Airport, and the Great Smoky Mountains National Park as examples of their work.

The Civil Works Administration and the Works Progress Administration mobilized community-centered projects that included building hundreds of schools, libraries, fire stations, playgrounds, skating rinks, and swimming pools.

The Federal Arts Projects sponsored murals for public buildings. The Federal Theatre Project enabled the performance of classical works to reach people in remote areas. The benefits of education, arts, and culture were a serious part of renewing and encouraging the members of our society.

This dynamic administration's chief aide believed... "that direct help in the form of a dole undermined character and independence and that men and women desperately wanted and needed the dignity of work and the discipline labor gave to one's life." I agree. It is clear that President Roosevelt believed giving a helping hand is a duty, not charity. That work must be done from the bottom up, not the top down, and that creativity, direct feedback, and flexibility were fundamental in administering these programs. He was also quick to cut the ones that didn't work.

I have listed what impressed me the most about these programs, which were aimed at developing individual character and dignity while working for the common good:

- They taught life skills.
- They taught fundamental health and hygiene skills.
- They taught social skills—how to live and work with a variety of other people.
- They taught practical skills, like how to handle one's money responsibly, to budget and support one's family or one's self.
- They taught respect for work and a spirit for working for goals beyond one's personal gain.
- They taught job skills.

These programs were considered an investment in our future, individually and collectively. In fact, they were an investment in our national character structure. As a boy I knew a number of men and women who had participated in some of these programs. They all considered them life-changing, often life-saving experiences, and they left them with a renewed sense of self-confidence and pride. They remembered them with gratitude and fondness.

In our country's history we have the model for how to give a hand up to our poor, support to people where jobs are in transition, and for a dynamic approach to challenges like global warming. But we must have the courage to renew this model in our times.

Unfortunately, the requirements for any program may seem too much for some people. There is a lesson for all of us in this reality. There never will be a helping-hand program that can change everyone. We must focus on helping and teaching the most people we can and understand our limits. Plus, no program can be put in place and then left unattended. All these types of programs are visions that must be lived into. They must be designed to evolve, to be re-imagined and changed with experience, as our society and workplace are changing over time.

*    *    *    *

Becoming a responsible citizen means learning how to face challenges and bounce back from stumbles and failures. It means learning how to become self-confident and self-disciplined and to delay self-gratification. Developing a basic sense of self-confidence comes from having goals, achieving them, and having that noticed. The combination of toughness, discipline, and support in the New Deal programs created a climate of enthusiasm, engagement, and the desire to be able to shape, direct, and improve one's life. We need to be teaching the people to whom we are giving a hand up today the competence and strength of character they need to become responsible adults and citizens. I can't help but think—wouldn't it be better if we focused as much on becoming responsible citizens as we do on the rights of citizens? Most of us have heard the old fable that says if you give a person a fish, you feed them for a day. If you teach a person to fish, they can feed themselves for a lifetime. It occurred to me when I was reading about the New Deal that while I am sure the Roosevelt administration faced many challenges and struggles, they were teaching their participants how to fish. Memories from my earlier years of working in the inner city came back to me while I was reading about those programs. Tears slowly filled my eyes. Tears of hope. During those violent, desperate years in my past, we were trying as hard as we could, and yet hope seemed beyond the horizon.

\* \* \* \*

We who have been living in the more affluent bubble the last few decades seem caught in a double bind. On the one hand, we want to be compassionate, or at least seem that way. On the other hand, we are afraid of and want to defend ourselves against the people, the culture, and the communities caught in the clutches of drastic economic hardships. We fear them as if we are being threatened by foreigners. We fear their crudeness, their potential violence, their anger, their drug use, their failure to know and respect our rules; most of all, far too many of us fear how much it might really cost to give them a helping hand. Well, all I can say is that, if we have learned anything at all from our history at home and abroad since World War II, it should be that whenever we allow ourselves to be driven down the path of fear, we are on a direct road to disaster. This is a time for us to help each other without fear and to invest in our country with creativity to rebuild the structure of our democracy, beginning with its human infrastructure.

\* \* \* \*

Inspired by the New Deal example from our history, I have to ask:
- Wouldn't it be better if we used this model on a larger scale to develop a program of teaching people to fish similar to the Works Progress Administration and the Civilian Conservation

Corps we had during the Great Depression?

- Wouldn't it be better if today's programs were founded on the development of character and resilience as well as job training?
- Wouldn't it be helpful to have a backbone in this program of trainers and teachers who were retired SEALs and the equivalent from other services—men and women who have learned to walk the walk of earning and living these values? Wouldn't it be helpful if these programs teach life skills, as the Marines taught them to J. D. Vance? This means to help one learn how to navigate in job markets, personal banking and shopping markets, the health care market, the insurance market, and others.
- Wouldn't it be better if today's programs include the basics of personal hygiene, nutrition, communication skills, and the need to understand and resist the fight-or-flight syndrome?
- Wouldn't it be better for us to realize that in today's world our programs must go beyond job training? Learning self-discipline, self-respect and self-responsibility teaches us to value ourselves and see our potentials. It also becomes the foundation that can support us in a rapidly changing world of jobs and economics.
- Wouldn't it be better if we devote a significant effort to develop the resources in our human infrastructure? These workers could revitalize our material infrastructure, work to conserve our natural resources, and work to boost our renewable energy industry. We would be lifting our ability to care for each other to a new level while at the same time fueling our economic engine.

This idea reminds me of Robert F. Kennedy's challenge to us in his great lecture on humanity: "We must do this, not because it is economically advantageous, although it is; not because the laws of God command it, although they do; not because people in other lands wish it so. We must do it for the single and fundamental reason that it is the right thing to do."

# NINE

—◆◆◆—

# ISN'T IT TIME TO STOP TREATING EACH OTHER AS IF WE ARE ENEMIES?

*Chaos begets chaos. Instability begets instability. Welcome to the family life of the American hillbilly.*

—*J. D. Vance*

Or more simply, welcome to our American political family.

"Winning is the only thing" may have been a successful theme for Vince Lombardi, long-time coach of the Green Bay Packers, a professional football team whose ability to make huge amounts of money depended on winning. But Lombardi's philosophy is incredibly destructive in politics, where the goals should be government of the people, by the people, and for the people. Of course, this attitude of winning is absolutely tragic in our relationships with each other, in our educational system, in business, and in nonprofessional sports—all

*Be right, win, trophy = Self esteem + narcissism*

areas where real leadership, character, and cooperation are truly needed.

As you can see, there are some things we need to wake up to and learn from this shipwreck of our ability to be civil to each other. The first thing we need to learn is that living in a world full of turmoil -- poverty, crime, violence, or more commonly, anxiety, tension, frustration, serious illness, and clashing parents and battling kids -- teaches our biology early on that we are in a scary world. We learn we can't feel safe or trust people to be good. Early in our lives our inner alarm system is programmed to be on high alert all the time. Without even realizing it we develop a way of life at a highly destructive level of stress.

Pay attention to the kind of personality J. D. Vance describes in *Hillbilly Elegy*. He points out that traumatic childhood events and their consequences are programmed into an individual and shapes them as adults. The events are called "adverse childhood experiences," or ACEs. Vance cites research reporting that well over half of the children of working-class adults have experienced such an event, and about 40 percent have had multiple ACEs. For children of professionals, the number is 29 percent. However, from my experience the percentage is much higher in impoverished areas and is more shockingly predominant in our total society than we are anywhere close to being aware of.

Vance goes on to explain the psychological genesis and effects of these events:

ACEs and their consequences reach far into adulthood. The trauma need not be physical. The following events or feelings are some of the most common ACEs:

- being sworn at, insulted, or humiliated by parents,

- being pushed, grabbed, or having something thrown at you,
- feeling that your family members don't support each other,
- having parents who are separated or divorced,
- living with an alcoholic or a drug user,
- living with someone who is depressed or has attempted suicide,
- watching a loved one be physically abused.

ACEs happen everywhere, in every community…

Children with multiple ACEs are more likely to struggle with anxiety and depression, to suffer from heart disease and obesity, and to contract certain types of cancers. They're also more likely to under-perform in school and suffer from relationship instability as adults. Even excessive shouting can damage a kid's sense of security and contribute to mental health and behavioral issues down the road.

Harvard pediatricians have studied the effects that childhood trauma have on the mind. In addition to negative health consequences, the doctors found that constant stress can actually change the chemistry of a child's brain.

Stress, after all, is triggered by a physiological reaction. It's the consequence of adrenaline and other hormones flooding our system, usually in response to some kind of stimulus. This is the classic fight-or-flight response we learn about in grad school. It sometimes produces incredible feats of strength and bravery from ordinary people.

J. D. Vance is telling us that growing up poor in harsh circumstances leaves us hard-wired for conflict. And that wiring remains until we change it, even when there is no more conflict. *Fight / flight super sensitive to be triggered.*

Now tell me what you think might happen when a policeman from a background similar to J. D. Vance's, one that programmed his reactions to be fight or flight, encounters a black teenager from a poor area that has the same fight-or-flight triggers combined with the propensity to use words as weapons.

*  *  *  *

Yes, people are programmed to behave this way without realizing the destructiveness of what they are doing. Much of the rage, rudeness, and misogyny we heard during the 2016 election reflected the outcry of people neurologically programmed this way. Yet it was also the roar of people who felt powerless, felt they didn't count, and felt that their values and lives were becoming worthless. Up to then they had felt "faceless." This reality doesn't mean we should accept threatening, destructive behavior. But we damn well better listen to what's behind it because it can get much worse. I can remember riots and burning cities in the late sixties.

I am irritated when politicians manipulate collective pain that has become a roar to their own ends, just as despicable demagogues have done in the past. The more I write about these realities the more powerless I feel, the more anger I feel, and the more I realize that today there is nothing tangible in our political parties that encourages me personally. During the election of 2016 I prayed, "Good Lord, please let this election be over!' But damn it all, it didn't stop on election day. The shit keeps hitting the fan.

Oh yes, maybe I'm beginning to understand. What if this rage and roar being expressed is a wounded cry of pain in reaction to the greed and indifference that we so readily accept in our society? What if they are the darkest expression of our collective indifference and ir-responsibility, surfacing as misogyny, neo-Nazism, or racial prejudice. It is much harder for us to look in the mirror, as Pogo the possum did in a comic strip fifty years ago, and say, "We have met the enemy and he is us." We damn well better pay attention to the rage around us and seek to understand it, so we do not fall into the trap of scape-goating these angry people, whether they are black, women, or "deplorable."

And guess what—as the world of working-class families tanks, so grow their fears of not being able to feed their children, not being able to take care of aging parents and seriously ill loved ones, and not being able to live in dignity in the face of disappearing standards of living. Stress levels and anger only increase with these fears. Consequently, the multiple ACEs for their children also increase. As do their levels of anxiety, depression, obesity, heart disease, autoimmune diseases, and certain kinds of cancer.

And guess what again—our more affluent families, the professional and upper-middle-class ones, also live at very high stress levels of anxiety and fear. They too, after the economic collapse in 2008, are worried about their financial safety and income security. Concerns about their children's school performance, college costs, aging parents, and shrinking health care coverage are eating them up. These households, too, are often filled with tension, and their members writhe in the grip of suppressed anger in the overworked, overstretched, overscheduled world of parents and kids. The families are suffering from angry outbursts—and their children are having their share of adverse childhood experiences which erode the foundation of their growing personali-

ties. They, too, can have fight, flight, or freeze patterned
into their brain. Underneath our tendency to appear in a
positive frame of mind, beneath our daily busyness, far
too many of us are stressed and scared and have trouble
admitting it.

How long have we been living in a toxic sea of
anxiety, depression, addictions and psychosomatic
illnesses? How long will it take us to realize stress makes
us sick?

## Are We Becoming Addicted to Anger, Despair, and Indifference?

Here are a few other points and questions you might
want to think about. Remember that J. D. Vance said
that due to fight, flight, or freeze reactions, "disagreements were war and you played to win the game."
Sounds like our national politics to me. Do you think
so many of us have become anxious and frustrated that
we have generally become indoctrinated into this fight,
flight, or freeze mentality? Do you think that treating
our political disagreements as war has become the
format for the "shouting heads" in our media and on
the internet? Remember when Crossfire appeared in the
nineties as the warfare-shouting model of political discussion? Now fast forward to our major news, radio
talk shows, and blogs today. Are we creating a self-per-
petuating cycle of fight, flight, or freeze in our world of
political discussions?

Whether it is intentional or not, our media has
learned to capitalize on how we experience ourselves
vicariously through it by keeping us revved up to the
point where our neurotransmitters such as norepineph-
rine, adrenaline, and dopamine are released, stimulating
our hearts and brains. As you see, we might want to

ask ourselves if our media in all its forms is attracting audiences by putting our emotions and acuity on high alert. Stop and listen. Can you imagine how easy it is today for people whose primary experience of life comes through the media to get physically addicted to it and emotionally controlled as well? The thrill, the rush—positive or negative—and the intensity of the hormones being released can be addictive even though they are propelling us into states of feeling hopeless, victimized, and enraged.

Well, I wonder, how does one of these shows or blogs make you feel? How did they make you feel during the presidential election period? Many people are learning to turn them off in disgust. But others are only paring them down to the ones that support their feelings, their emotional perspective, that help them feel validated. But far too many of us end up ready to go into a hyper-emotional state whenever politics are even mentioned. And there are also those of us who have been conditioned to freeze rather than to tell others they are temporarily insane.

As for the answers to these questions, I am still left wondering how much of our arousal is due to our conditioning growing up and how much is caused by or simply manipulated by the media. In any event, we cannot be a healthy society and be driven by an addicting media. We must not let ourselves slip into the trap of letting media politics or politicians continue to take advantage of and exacerbate our fears, frustrations, and weaknesses the way demagogues have throughout history.

In the 2016 presidential election, we saw that a nonvote is a vote, and a vote to say to-hell-with-you-all is also a vote. But unless we wake up and take action to change, we will continue to feel betrayed by our system and our government—defrauded and alone. This result is tragic. We can do better.

I wonder how long it is going to take us to learn to love life and care for each other. When I say love, I don't mean the usual sentimental mush or sex-driven movie scenes. I mean a condition in the human spirit so profound that it encourages us to develop courage; I mean the courage to put in the kinds of solutions I am writing about. I mean the courage to build bridges, to reach out to other people and to help them better their lives.

# TEN

# HEALTH CARE: ISN'T IT TIME TO QUIT BEING THE CRUELEST DEVELOPED NATION?

*We are rightly proud of the high standards of medical care we know how to provide in the U.S. The fact is, however, that most of our people cannot afford to pay for the care they need. I have often and strongly urged that this condition demands a national health program. The heart of the program must be a national system of payment for medical care based on well-tried insurance principles. This great nation cannot afford to allow its citizens to suffer needlessly for the lack of proper medical care.*

*—Harry S. Truman*

*I have had some bitter disappointments as president, but the one that has troubled me most, in a personal way, has been the failure to defeat opposition to a national compulsory health insurance program.*

*—Harry S Truman*

How can I begin to write about my country -- the country where I grew up, the country that has given me a lot, the country I love, that I am a patriot in -- as the cruelest developed nation in the world? The only way I know is to begin with a story. This is the story of three generations of my family's relationship to our health-care system. These are stories of suffering, struggle, and grief. They molded the lives of my family members. But I'm not telling them as tales of woe. I'm telling them to show the human side, my experience, my family's experience of the financial costs of health care, and the cross these costs crucify us on. And for the first time I'm going to let my inner deplorables—my shadow side, long repressed—speak on the page.

If you look around you, in your own family, among your friends, relatives, neighbors, colleagues at work, fellow church members, all the people around you, you will see plenty of stories like mine. In our addiction to positive thinking, we have let ourselves come to believe that being happy and healthy is normal. It is not. Chronic, acute, and temporary illnesses, accidents, and death are touching us all the time. Perhaps it is our denial that allows us to be so cruel. In my professional practice as well as in my personal life, I have grown very aware of how many people, often quietly, too quietly in our society, are suffering from intense illness, physical, psychic, and emotional pain, every moment of the day.

In 2016, a total of 2,744,248 resident deaths were registered in the United States, according to the Centers for Disease Control. Of those people 155,800 died of cancer. Cancer—there is no good way to die of cancer. It is a long, torturous, terrifying journey for patients, for loved ones, and often for caregivers as well. Accidental injury claimed 47,800 lives and caused many more serious injuries. While these statistics demand attention, our real attention must stay with the knowledge that they represent the deaths of real people—people who loved, feared, hurt, dreamed, hated what's happening, and wanted to have whatever care and security they could get. And they wanted the same for their spouses, partners, children, loved ones, or even for the person in the next hospital or nursing home bed. They are people like those in my stories.

## Story Number One

Shortly after World War II, when I was around ten, a vivacious baby girl was born into our family. She brought joy to the eyes of my parents and into all our hearts as we were starting a new life after the war. One afternoon she was sitting on the edge of our dining room table after a swim in her little two-piece swimsuit. Laughing and waving her arms, she entertained us and some family friends. Suddenly, my mother's face became deadly serious. She had noticed a lump on my sister's side that took the smiles off everyone's faces.

Our friends stayed with us until our doctor arrived. Soon my sister was in the hospital and being operated on for a Wilms cancer tumor on her kidney. I was only a child at the time and it took me decades, until I was in my professional training, to imagine the ongoing terror that must have seized the heart of that little girl who had been cut open from her backbone to her belly button to have her kidney removed. But I could see the anguish in my parents' eyes and the bitter tears they shed at night as they prayed for her life. Helplessly they had to watch their baby suffer and could not even cradle her in their arms for many days. There wasn't much in the way of health insurance in those days, but my parents weren't considering costs because action was needed. But the costs caught up with us. They hovered around us like a cloud, haunting our family, causing fear and stress until they were finally paid.

## Story Number Two

Shortly after my sister's recovery, my mother was diagnosed with breast cancer. Like so many women, she suffered a long, harrowing journey of multiple surgeries and crude (at that time) radiation treatments. She died a painful death in 1952 when she was forty-two. I was fourteen and devastated, as were we all. This journey had lasted four years, and there was no hospice then. My father put a hospital bed in their bedroom and slept on a single bed next to her every night. For the last three months, we had two shifts of nurses every day.

When she died, my father was left with three shattered children, a broken heart, and a mountain of debt. He had to sell the dream home they had bought after the war. He was a good man, and he turned to hard work to care for us and to pay off the debt. It took him almost fifteen years to pay it off, and I know he had to deal with several threatened lawsuits along the way. During those years, as if the debt was an ongoing reminder of his broken heart, I saw a vital part of his spirit close down and become inaccessible to us. Learning that tragedy and debt can easily combine to sap our spirit and wall off our capacity to be open and loving is a harsh lesson.

## Story Number Three

When I was a junior at Georgia Tech, I went to a French-themed party at my fraternity house after a football game. As I walked into the bar area of the party room, I saw a young woman sitting at the bar in a jaunty beret and a sexy black dress with a split skirt. As she talked, she radiated vivacity and humor. When we danced, her eyes sparkled. We were married during my senior year and had our son the week I graduated. Over the next few years, we had two daughters. To tell the truth, we had both experienced anguished childhoods and, in a sense, were lost children who dreamed of creating a perfect family. We worked very hard in that direction. When my wife was in her late twenties, I noticed she was struggling at times with herself and her feelings. But I was working hard and wasn't very psychologically minded at the time. I suggested she go back to school, and she did.

A few years later, she became almost totally inactive, lying on the sofa most of the day, weeping at times, and pouring her heart into her journals. Our family doctor suggested we see a psychiatrist and gave us a referral. I was stunned, but my wife seemed full of hope that she might be understood and helped. We went into his office where he sat in a coat and tie behind a huge desk. After we relayed to him a brief history, he asked me to leave the room so he could talk with her. As I was leaving, I saw her handing him her journals.

After about half an hour, she came out looking like she had shrunk a whole size. His secretary asked me to go in. I sat down in front of him. He leaned back in his chair and said to me in a gruff voice, "Hell, man, she's psychotic. She needs to be in the hospital." Then he tossed her journals across the desk at me and said, "Have you read this stuff? It's schizophrenic!" Well, to be honest with you, in 1970 I didn't know what schizophrenic meant. But I had read some of her journals and knew what pain and struggle looked like. What he said temporarily shocked me into immobility, which was good because I would have done him bodily harm for his crass response to me and someone I loved.

However, I followed up on his advice and went to visit the Georgia Mental Health Institute, which was a psychiatric hospital in Atlanta with a good reputation. It was also a teaching hospital for Emory University, which had the reputation of having the finest medical school in the state. The staff was very kind, and they showed me around the hospital, which was actually a group of large cottages (units) connected by underground tunnels and having grassy courtyards. Paradoxically, I actually did an internship there some years later.

The staff explained that their treatment approach was "rapid tranquilization" (common and popular at the time), which amounted to sedating the patients and bringing them under control. I thought to myself that this simply turned their patients into zombies. My wife wasn't having violent fits, and I couldn't see putting someone I loved into this situation or kind of treatment. So, I thanked them, left, and earnestly began to look for other options.

This has been the hardest story of all for me to remember and to tell. I find it hard to revisit. My memories are foggy; I don't want to remember these very hard times.

The following years were filled with pain and struggle. Yet there were many happy moments with my kids. It took me decades to recall that it wasn't all hell with my wife; there were happy moments with her, too. We eventually found the Atlanta Psychiatric Clinic, which was a cutting-edge clinic of top psychiatrists and psychologists who were deeply versed in a humanistic approach to the human psyche, the soul, and psycho-therapy. Even though my wife was diagnosed schizophrenic, drugs were never suggested. We initially went for therapy two or three times per week. The therapy passed the decade mark and went on.

I know our life was very turbulent, scary at times, harrowing at other times, but I believe what we did added years of real living to her life and gave our children a better experience of her than they would have had otherwise. Let me tell you, though, that what made those years seem like a total hell was having my back to the wall financially, day after day, with no end in sight. This damnable pressure robbed me of being able to enjoy our kids in the way I wish I could have, of loving them the way I really wanted to, and of being there for them the way I wish I could have been when they needed me. It also caused me to lose my temper at times that I now regret. Eventually, it all became too much, and I had my own period of collapse which included a divorce.

## Story Number Four

In the year 2004, my daughter was diagnosed with progressive multiple sclerosis. Hers was a young family, with three children in the house and a husband who owned his own small business. That year put them on a chilling roller coaster ride that is still continuing. If I tried to describe it, I would choke up and lose my ability to write. But they continue to meet the demands—all of them, with love, courage, and resilience. But what I can tell you is from the day she was diagnosed until the day the Affordable Care Act passed, they were stuck in being unable to change their health insurance. The medical bills that weren't covered by their insurance ran into the middle five figures, year after year. They were able to change policies after the Affordable Care Act passed, but their monthly premium is still over $3,000 a month, and they still have to pay deductibles and co-pays.

Can you imagine what this kind of financial pressure does to a family when it combines with such a severe illness in a loved member? Ten thousand new cases of MS are diagnosed every year—about 200 per week, and the number is growing. Are we going to continue to abandon our most vulnerable citizens, our loved ones, to a financial hell while they are caught in the relentless undertow of this basic reality of life?

## The Rage and the Pain

Terrorists rely on making us live in fear of what's going to happen next. We wait, we expect, we anticipate, and we imagine…and always the worst. Living in the face of a serious illness -- where every decision is made based on health needs or governed by costs or by whether the finest doctor is an in-network provider -- is another kind of terrorism. I know the terror, and I weep burning tears for the unnecessary suffering of three generations of my family—my parents, my wife and me, and our children—and the millions like us. I say "unnecessary" because President Harry S. Truman, one of our most practical and honest presidents, proposed to Congress a new national health-care act in 1945. Enacting it would have saved all three generations of my family plus millions of other American families from the needless financial crunch that drained too much of our capacity to love and care for each other in some of life's darkest moments.

I am so angry, angry, angry that words of profanity expressing my anger don't even come to me. My shadow, my inner deplorable, is wild with the rage I've denied at the members of our Congress—sitting there in their cocoons of health-care security for over seventy-three years. For all that time, they have been carrying on about such issues as government interference, deficits, taxes, statistics, and stuff like that while the people in my family, my friends, and many of the people I work with are being crucified on a cross of medical bills, treatment choices, and financial despair that scorches the soul of someone who is trying to cope with some of life's blackest moments.

Senators and representatives, where are your hearts? But I must also ask, "Where have the hearts been of those who elected you...where has my heart been?"

I am an American and I believe in competition in the right places. We are number one in health costs per capita in the developed nations. But according to the World Health Organization, the U.S. is ranked number thirty-seven in the world for its level of health care and education. Please tell me, Mr. or Ms. Congressperson, what are we competing at here?

I can't help but wonder why it is so easy for us to lie to ourselves and each other. For example, calling a single-payer system "socialized medicine" is perpetuating a term coined by a major advertising agency that the American Medical Association, fearing change and loss of control of the health-care market, hired to combat President Truman's proposal. As I said previously, when we follow the road of fear, we generally end up on the road to disaster. In a true socialized-medicine situation, the government pays the bills, owns the health-care facilities, and employs the professionals who work there. Our Veterans Administration health system is a socialized health system run by the government.

Some time ago, a physician client of mine said he felt very guilty because he could afford my services and yet many of his patients who badly needed this kind of help could not. That is part of the very problem I'm talking about. In most developed countries, people's health plans would cover my services. In general, the term single-payer means that all medical claims are paid out of a government-run pool of money. Under this plan, all providers are paid equally, and patients receive the same benefits regardless of their ability to pay. A single-payer fund can include a public health-care delivery system, a private delivery system, and a mix of the two, such as I have with my Medicare and Medicare supplemental policies. When I lived in Europe, I learned that most European countries had a wide range of supplementary policies one could buy, similar to the wide range of Medicare supplemental policies I can buy through private companies here in the U.S.

A shameful part of our Medicare history has been that Congress reserves the right to limit provider fees. Too often it seems to me they have kept the fees low as a political manipulation to turn providers against the system. Another shameful aspect of this problem is that we fail to educate ourselves and our American family about what a single-payer program really means. It ensures access to medical care for everyone. This fact alone means that the prevention of disease and the promotion of healthy living will have a major focus. It means, and tears well up when I think of this point, that the fear of medical bankruptcy or of making a wrong decision because of finances or simply living in financial terror might no longer be an issue.

A big part of the shame is the lies we are told and the lies we believe that come from people with a vested interest, such as insurance companies and their lobbyists. The for-profit health-care industry is quick to tell us we will lose the freedom to choose our plan and to choose our doctor. Well, guess what? We lost those freedoms long ago. What if the doctor or specialist you want is not on your insurance company's network provider list? This happened to my daughter. As for choosing your own plan—if you have an employer, that's done for you and generally to your employer's advantage. Anyone naïve enough to think that buying a plan on an open competitive market is a good idea should take a look at all the complicated medical terms, legalese, and exclusions in every plan. Thinking the average American could make an informed choice on the open market is simply a cruel joke.

There are almost too many lies perpetuated in our national debate on health care for me to even discuss. "Death panels" were a lie. Another lie is that care will deteriorate or cost a lot more. Really? Remember, we are already thirty-seventh in care but first in costs—far ahead of all the other countries that have single-payer plans and better care than us.

*  *  *  *

Even as I finish my reflections, I have to ask myself these questions:
- Wouldn't it be better if we face the truth that we, the majority of our citizenry, want to stop the financial horror that accompanies illness in this country and adopt a single-payer system?
- Wouldn't it be better if everyone with a disease or illness is treated, and prevention and healthy living are promoted?
- Wouldn't it be better if we challenge ourselves to become the number one country in the world in health care?

- Wouldn't it be better to be the world's leader in promoting an environment that doesn't make us sick?

## The Bedrock of Cruelty

It is incredible how deaf, dumb, and blind we are to nonphysical pain. If you break a leg, have cancer, the flu, or some other disease, people sympathize and want to help you. They show you respect. If you are in an area where a hurricane has trashed everything, people rush in with boats, food, shelter, and all sorts of help. But if you are paralyzed with despair, scared to get out of bed, can't see a reason for living, have lost hope, or are just sinking into a swamp of bitterness and misery, it almost seems like no one can help you—or in fact really wants to try to help you. Plus, our addiction to positive thinking enables wholesale denial of the amount of psychological suffering around us, and perpetuates our view of it as a personal, embarrassing, and humiliating failure.

And, you may be sure that seeing how much the profession I entered with enthusiasm, hard-earned educational credentials, and the hope to make lives better has been marginalized fills me with the kind of anger that better helps me understand other angry people in political rallies. Perhaps we are angry at a society we feel has marginalized us.

Statistics tell us that on average, 129 of our fellow Americans kill themselves every day. An estimated 88,000 die of alcohol-related causes every year. There were more than 70,000 deaths from drug overdoses in 2017. My daily news sources bombard me with the severity of the opioid crisis we are now having throughout our country.

I believe there is an important story behind these statistics. When I did much of my training during the 1970s and early 1980s, a lot of attention was being given to mental health and treatment, and to the dramatically increasing rate of depression and anxiety in our country. Mental health was well covered by insurance plans in the 1980s, and it was recognized that every dollar spent on mental health saved three dollars in other medical, law enforcement, and social costs.

When I and my current wife, who is also a Jungian psychoanalyst, moved back to America in 1989 after our analytic training in Zurich, Switzerland, we chose to live in Asheville, North Carolina. Asheville is a beautiful mountain town that I had been familiar with since childhood, and I had always seen North Carolina as a progressive state (I don't mean in current political terms, but in reality). When we arrived here, we found a very active state-supported mental health system. The offices in Asheville were welcoming and well-staffed by psychiatrists, psychologists, social workers, and supporting staff. Counseling and therapy were available for adults, couples, families, adolescents, and children on a sliding scale depending upon income. This system was supported by two private psychiatric hospitals in the city, two solid addiction treatment programs, and a supporting network of private practitioners. My wife and I were glad to join this climate of professionalism and caring.

By the year 2000, all these facilities were gone—the state facilities, the psychiatric hospitals, the addiction treatment programs, and many of the supporting professionals. What happened to these programs fills me with a cold rage—a rage that eliminates my detachment and any chance of forgiveness. Where did they go, you might wonder? The answer is that "managed care" came on the scene. Under the rubric of cutting medical costs and delivering "better care," the true focus was on increasing profits. *Greed - ultimate addiction*

Too many people have bought the illusion that therapy or counseling shows weakness and that all it consists of is vomiting one's feelings. These are destructive fictions. North Carolina's former facilities had the purpose of helping people to build a foundation for living productively and responsibly, to build skills, to break out of loneliness—which our research shows kills us. Those mental health systems were meant to help citizens find hope, direction, and the capacity to love, and to make a contribution to society. They were meant to express our caring for each other and our compassion for the truly mentally ill so they could live in dignity, and their families could live securely.

The reality was this. If some man or woman was drowning in despair, anger, or confusion, if some teenage boy or girl was struggling to stay afloat, or some couple or family was caught in the riptides of modern life, if someone was caught in a hurricane of addictions, there was a safe harbor—a place to find care and support. Such a harbor gives support to the whole community. It gives parents, teachers, ministers, and even the police a feeling of security that facilitates empathy, caring for each other, and civility. It does so because we know our backs are covered if we pay attention, listen to each other, and get involved.

Because they address nonphysical pain that people prefer to be blind to, mental health benefits were an easy area in which to start cutting costs. Using the "managed care" method, the health insurance companies made getting treatment approvals so limited, so tedious, and so obnoxious that our delivery system buckled, and many of our best providers either quit taking insurance or left the field altogether while our politicians, professional associations, and the media turned a blind eye to what was going on. The public simply focused on the illusion that things were getting better and tried to appear happy, an approach to life that fosters denial. (Once again, check out Barbara Ehrenreich's *Bright-Sided*.)

Our mental health care system is very broken, and we have lost a critical support system that we badly need in a culture that is being driven by fear, anxiety, and anger. I have kept too much anger locked inside of me. I am very angry that so many people in this new opioid epidemic really have no place to go for help. I'm even angrier that all the places they could have gone to for help or treatment to ward off the pressures or problems that lead to addiction are simply no longer here. And I am ashamed of our politicians, and I am ashamed of all of us for letting this cruel tragedy happen in our society.

\* \* \* \*

When I began my professional training in psychology in the early seventies, the atmosphere of the field was still dominated by the work of the great humanistic psychologist Carl Rogers. He was a man whose work was governed by depth and kindness, including his groundbreaking book *Becoming a Person*. Rogers taught that to become a person, we must know ourselves. We must confront and know our shadow, our darkness, our rage, and our shame. And we must know the goodness and strength within ourselves that we have repressed, because to have lived them would have made us different from the crowd—noticed, embarrassed, perhaps even criticized.

But we must face these parts of ourselves and learn from them. It is only from this foundation that we can live into the realizations of truly new potentials, restore old worlds, and recognize new horizons. Becoming a person in this way is also the best foundation for becoming a good citizen, a person who acts responsibly to nourish and energize our government as one of the people, by the people, and for the people.

I pray that we can face our cruelty as our forebears faced their darkest hours and find again America's strength. This strength has been our ability to stand up to any challenge, no matter how difficult and daunting. Isn't it time that we accept our challenge to create the number one health-care system in the world, one that considers and treats every citizen as sacred?

Absence of love leads to Addiction, suicide, Violence or Power, greed, Control — The absence of empathy, Connection, Community in place of individuation. We cannot measure the most important parts of our lives is our meaning + purpose + our relationship of intimacy.

# ELEVEN

# 2008: BETRAYAL AS ANOTHER WAKE-UP CALL

*I swore never to be silent whenever and wherever human beings endure suffering and humiliation. We must always take sides. Neutrality helps the oppressor, never the victim. Silence encourages the tormentor, never the tormented.*

—Elie Wiesel

During the 9-11 commission hearings, the former national coordinator for anti-terrorism, Richard Clarke, took the stand and made the most amazing public statement I have ever seen or heard from a government official. He began his interview with an apology to the victims of 9-11 and their loved ones. He then said, "Your government failed you, those entrusted with your protection failed you, and I failed you." This scene was an expression of character like none I have ever seen anywhere or anytime in our government.

I don't in any way equate 9-11 with the economic crash in 2008, but just as our entire nation was affected by the 9-11 attacks, our whole nation was victimized by the 2008 crash. Countless people sank into a sea of poverty, lost their jobs, declared bankruptcy, and committed suicide. A *Wall Street Journal* article on January 27, 2018, pointed out that about 2.5 million homes are still worth less than their mortgage debt—ten years later. My children and their families felt a kind of fear and dread they had never known before, although I had. No one in the government that was supposed to have protected us took responsibility for this tragedy the way Richard Clarke had done for 9-11. No one in our government apologized for letting greed become more important than your and my welfare and that of other citizens—their constituents. No one in our government apologized for having repealed the Glass-Steagall Act, which had been the firewall protecting us from predatory financial institutions since the Great Depression. And no one in the Justice Department took action to prosecute the people who had robbed me and my family of the security we had worked so hard to attain to support our later years. I was punched in the stomach and brought to my knees, and I wasn't anywhere near the only one.

*No accountability*

If my government couldn't protect me, I wish it would have at least pursued justice. I would have liked to have seen those reckless, greedy bastards who pocketed billions punched in the gut themselves by our Justice Department. I would have liked to have seen them go to jail, like people in the savings and loan scandals did in the early 1990s. The very people in our government who should have been protecting us from greedy predators were and are facilitating them. Instead of making high-paid speeches on Wall Street, I would have liked to have heard 2016 Democratic presidential candidate Hillary Clinton chanting, "Lock 'em up! Lock 'em up!"

in her campaign rallies. This whole situation is so damn painful! I am full of rage and pain and heartbreak by our indifference that has allowed so many members of Congress to easily sell us out to stay in office.

\* \* \* \*

I have lived on a slippery slope financially more than once in my life. But I was taking financial risks for purposes I valued—medical treatments for my family members, starting a new business, and responding to a call to a new vocation. During these times I was confident in what I was doing and had faith that if I stumbled or fell, I could pick myself up again, which I had to do several times. This time, in 2008 and 2009, it was different. I was blindsided, a bottom dropped out from under me that I hadn't even realized was there.

We remodeled our home in 2007 to be a place where we could live for a long time. It was spacious enough for our children and their families to be able to visit with us on holidays and special occasions. When we finished remodeling, it appraised for a high enough value to reassure us that we had some bedrock financial security as we faced the future. In 2008, I turned seventy-one years old and was still working, as I am now. In one fell swoop, we lost the foundation of financial security we had in our home and more than I like to think about in our retirement funds. Everyone we knew was seized by a state of shock and fear. Within a couple of years, we realized we needed to bite the bullet, dump our beautiful home at a huge loss, and drastically downsize. We did it. We are tough, creative, and courageous. Plus, we made this drastic change in our lives while I was recovering from surgery for prostate cancer.

I have a great deal of respect for myself, for my wife, and for others who hung in there, endured, cared for their loved ones, and quietly dealt with their fear and grief. I also have so much compassion for all who had hopes and dreams smashed, who lost everything, and who faced poverty and serious illnesses as their finances collapsed. Almost nine million people lost their jobs, five million families lost their homes, and the unemployment rate doubled to around 10 percent. And I damn well hate the people who brought on this debacle along with the self-serving politicians who forgot they actually have a responsibility to protect the people who elected them.

Bitterness wells up in my throat when I remember that our two main candidates for president in 2016 both sit snugly in the top one percent of wealth; that they are clearly connected with the powers on Wall Street. I am amazed at how easily they thought their rhetoric and bombastic statements could deceive us. I make these comments with pain and anguish because I believe the Democratic candidate has tried to do good for children, women, health care, and the world many times, but I have to ask, "What in the world, Madame Secretary, could you have believed I would think when you took a $600,000 check for one of four speeches on Wall Street (of which you didn't release the contents) and then tried to appear like you had my interests at heart in your campaign speeches? On top of that, I can't help but wonder if you are so out of touch that it didn't occur to you that it would take a single mother supporting a couple of kids as a waitress almost thirty years to make that much money. Come on!" The other candidate took the Gordon Gekko approach, which charismatically suggests, at least to some people, that greed, self-interest, and uncontrolled power are good.

Another realization that hit me like a punch in the stomach was the recognition that when the bottom line in a woman's life is winning power, money, and prestige at any cost, she is actually a member of the predatory patriarchy. She has adopted the same value structure that is destroying the humanity in our society, no matter what kind of feminist persona she is wearing.

Being a one-percenter, however, doesn't make you evil. The politicians that inspire me the most, Theodore Roosevelt, Franklin Roosevelt, Eleanor Roosevelt, and Robert Kennedy, for example, were one-percenters but lived by the values of wanting to lift our lives to higher purposes and meanings. Other heroes of mine such as Harry S. Truman, George Marshall, Martin Luther King, Jr., and even Mother Teresa knew very well how to have, create, and use power and not be corrupted by the pursuit of it.

In his book *The Power Paradox: How We Gain and Lose Influence*, Dacher Keltner, Ph.D., shares with us his research on power. He says when people who are seeking power or who have power lose focus on others it "can lead to empathy deficits and the loss of compassion, impulsive and unethical action, and rude and uncivilized behavior." He notes that someone feeling powerful and going in a negative direction can lead to assumptions of entitlement and being above the law. But not all wealthy or powerful people are like this. Wealth and power can also lead to an increased desire to serve the good of others and a deepened sense of empathy and compassion, as embodied by the people I've named.

## "Indifference to me is the epitome of evil."

Where in the world was my brain, my public

awareness, as we were laying the political groundwork leading up to 2008? The quotation I am using as the title of this section comes from the Nobel Prize winner and former Nazi concentration camp victim Elie Wiesel. It came to my mind while I was reading a passage in Joe Biden's book *Promise Me, Dad*. He was describing taking his granddaughter to tour Dachau, the former Nazi concentration camp. I have toured Dachau myself, and it is a picture of hell. Former Vice-President Biden writes that his father reminded him that "the idea that the German people did not know this was happening defied logic. Humans are capable of incredible cruelty, our father wanted me, my sister, and my brothers to understand. And just as dangerous, he made us see, human beings are also capable of looking the other way and remaining silent when awful things are happening all around them."

Well, guess what, Mr. Vice President, haven't most of our politicians, too many of our business leaders, our medical and psychological professional societies, most of us—and I, myself—been living in denial of the hell too many of our fellow citizens are experiencing? Everyone in the bubble of indifference is helping to make denial a national psychological defense mechanism. It predominates in liberal circles that have been supported by our obsessive dogma of positive thinking. Denial is an attempt to screen out difficult and unpleasant realities by ignoring them or refusing to acknowledge them.

A large portion of our society that tends to be conservative goes further and uses repression as a psychological defense mechanism. In repression, threatening or painful thoughts, events, and realities are excluded from our awareness. Like all defense mechanisms, these two are used to protect us from anxiety, from recognizing the fear we are living in. They also protect us from facing the encapsulated way we are living, which prevents us finding the courage to confront our true reality and its unpleasant demand to become more self-responsible in our actions. Former Vice- President Biden ends his passage by saying, "You can't remain silent. Silence is complicity." I agree, and that is why I am compelled to write this book that is challenging me every minute while I am engaged with it.

\*   \*   \*   \*

While too many of us were living in denial and buying the illusion that things were getting better, they were actually getting worse for too many people and were, in fact, getting much worse for all of us, more than we realized. Our denial equals indifference, and our failure to face reality is casting a dark shadow over our national power structure and our lifestyles. Indifference blurs the lines between good and evil. (Elie Wiesel gives a great talk on indifference. You can view it on YouTube.) Indifference makes it easier to look away from victims, our neighbors, and reduces them to abstractions, statistics, and political groups. I'm sick of hearing Democrats say, for example, that they lost the 2016 election because they failed to reach out to blue-collar workers. I just want to scream, "Son of a bitch, you didn't reach out to me, you didn't inspire me, and I'm not a blue-collar worker!"

Maybe, just maybe, so-called blue-collar workers and I have a deeper set of concerns and values in common than you realize. Maybe they include the values of the heart. Maybe they include wanting a government that is on our side—that is of the people, by the people, and for the people. Maybe they include standing for the fundamental values of democracy, liberty, equality, and opportunity for all of us. And I would like to mention: quit trying to assume or convince me I have these things, because the punch in the gut I received in 2008 proved to me that I don't. Indifference to suffering makes us inhuman. Indifference to the victims of 2008 makes us a friend of the enemies of democracy. In the years leading up to 2008, my humanity was denied by my government. My citizenship was denied by the perpetrators of that disaster, but also by my president, my senators, my representatives, our political parties, and the new presidential candidates.

Elie Wiesel says that "it is remembering that will save humanity." He says also that when the American soldiers liberated him from the concentration camp, he could see the shock, the horror, and the compassion in their eyes. He said that he was comforted because he knew they would never forget. We must never forget that we were devastatingly betrayed in 2008 and got a shocking wake-up call in 2016 because we have forgotten that in this country, this democracy, we are meant to be self-aware, self-responsible citizens and not subjects of a power structure. And we must remember that those who seek power and money for their own sake are still directing our lives. Once again, I have to ask:

- Wouldn't it be better if we remember that we do have power? Communication, protest, and voting are power!
- And wouldn't it be better if we remember that the forces that want to undermine a government of the people, by the people, and for the people thrive on us believing that we don't have enough power, that we can't make a difference so there is no reason to act?

# PART IV

---·◆·---

## Reclaiming Our Founding Dream

*We the people are the rightful Masters of both Congress and the courts, not to overthrow the Constitution but to overthrow the men who pervert the Constitution.*

—*Abraham Lincoln*

# TWELVE

———— •✦• ————

# POWER UP: RECLAIMING THE HEART OF OUR DEMOCRACY

*The future is worth fighting for. The dreams of our forebears are worth defending. The aspirations of our children are worth protecting. And the American Dream itself is worth reinventing— and rebuilding. We have a duty to stand up to the dream-killers in our country.*

—*Van Jones*

That deep muse within me that expresses my heart has driven me to write this book. The truth is that she connects me to my heart. She wants me to see through my heart's eyes, to hear through my heart's ears, and to live with my heart as my guide. She confronts me with the questions of why I don't want to open my eyes and ears, of why I don't want to open my heart. She knows that if I do, my heart will want to cut through our cultural chaos and rely on common sense. She knows that as I open, as I have been writing, my heart will scream with anger at the realities I see and feel chagrin at my previous indifference and blindness. She also knows I will face a moral challenge, which is to speak out honestly, as I am trying my best to do in these reflections. To have gotten this far in my writing is to have accepted her challenge.

When I wrote about being in the sixth grade in an area of rural poverty, I mentioned the bullies, the predators in the school. Around bullies, we learn how to keep to ourselves, be quiet, and try to avoid being noticed so we won't be threatened or hurt. The paradox is that our passivity enables the bullies. The same is true in our adult world and the world of social institutions that have become bullies in many situations. Bullies can be found in the top one percent of wealthy families, in major corporations, and in our governing bodies. These predators are running our lives. The heart of power today is hard. The predators have controlled our elections on many levels. A wealthy enough family (or corporation) can buy a congressperson or a majority in a state legislature.

Giant corporations can spend enough money to create or sway legislators or to prevent legislation that is in the country's best interests. They can marshal the media power to sell us lies such as that the Affordable Care Act will create "death panels," or we will lose the freedom to choose our doctor or, worst of all, to label it "Obamacare" in order to denigrate and associate it with racial prejudice. Deep in my heart I am so angry! But, that's not even close to all of the story. The big health insurance bullies use the hard-earned money we pay in premiums not on our health-care costs but by the millions, maybe billions, to flood us with propaganda and our legislatures with lobbying efforts that are against

*Power & wealth*

our best interests. Then, if our eyes are open, we see the predators are rearranging the laws and government regulations meant to "protect" us to their advantage. For the predators, might makes right, and they want the law of the jungle to become the law of the land.

As these predators become more institutionalized, they seem to become more accepted, even expected. In the 2016 election, we even seemed to appreciate some of them as they pushed and supported candidates.

As furious as I am with the predators, I know their existence reflects a deeper crisis we need to face that is more than just an economic or political problem. We are losing the heart and soul of our tradition, of the American spirit, and of our democracy. An attitude of narrow self-interest, hard-hearted practicality, and short-term vision is wreaking havoc across our land. It shows little concern for people's actual well-being, it diminishes imagination and thoughtfulness, and it brands a passion for truth and knowledge as irrelevant. In the world I was born into, which was by no means a perfect world, more of our citizens cared about each other. More of them cared about our government being an instrument of that care, protecting and empowering us all through public provisions. Good God! Just remembering that no other advanced political society has the amount of poverty we have drives me nuts!

We have become so driven, busy, and scared that we have let the values of the heart in our society, for ourselves and everyone else, fade into the background of our lives. When our values of the heart fade, they leave an empty space inside us that feeds on feelings of fear and scarcity and evolves into a quest for possessions, money, and security or power. Then we become the victims of these needs and the forces they arouse.

*Heart values ask for vulnerability to face possible rejection & fear of not enough*

In writing this most difficult book I found it was a challenge to open my eyes to look in the mirror and see how much I feared giving up my denial and indifferences and how much it might cost me. Well, destiny fixed that problem by turning my world upside down with our political chaos. It knocked the props out from under me and made me able to see with more clarity and honesty the reality I'm living in and that I must help change.

## Our Democracy Is Weak

I have spent four decades thinking of myself as a pretty good citizen. I am law-abiding. I vote, pay my taxes, look after my family, contribute to charities, and care about my community. Now my new awakening is forcing me to ask myself, "How could I have been sleep-walking through the last four decades, minimizing my awareness of the predators and the sliding of my government and my fate into their hands?" I don't believe I expected myself—or we expected each other—to aspire to the core principles of citizenship, of taking self-responsibility and collective responsibility, of cultivating the inner capacity to know what rings true. In fact, down deep, I knew a lot of the rhetoric and political posturing didn't ring true. But I tended to brush it off rather than try to step beyond the lies, express my outrage, and take action.

During those four decades, far too many of us deluded ourselves into thinking we were living in a sincere and active democracy ruled by freedom of thought and opinion. But as I have been pursuing these reflections, I have come to know that in my heart I didn't really believe these assumptions were true and rage was accumulating.

In my own shadow, I was aware that our democracy

was weak and becoming weaker. Plus, our democracy was idle because we were idle. Other politically advanced nations have had a much higher percentage of voter turn-out than we have had for most of these forty years. As our democracy has weakened, we have become increasingly ruled by predators and fear. We are afraid of taking risks, of speaking out, of being criticized, of not being politically correct, of being confronted, of offending family, friends, neighbors, and of losing business. Have we become afraid of being free? Freedom requires taking risks, taking stands, and having courage. It requires calling a lie a lie when it is necessary. It requires standing up to people who have become so afraid that they have become despotic in their political positions and are forgetting that the lives of every one of our citizens is sacred. The predators and people who promote the despotic political positions are ignoring the body politic and are attacking the soul of our democracy.

I think that it is clear we are by far the most militarily powerful country on the earth. I don't fear anything outside of this country, not terrorism, or wild dictators, or floods of immigrants. What I fear most of all is the number of our citizens that are becoming dehumanized and alienated, the weakening of our democracy. I am afraid that if we are not careful, we are condemning ourselves to a civil death while we are distracting ourselves with a fear of outside forces.

I am also afraid of the attack on truth in our media and in politics. I have to state this trend because it scares me so much, and others are writing books about this problem. I am also ashamed that we think we are the land of opportunity. We are not what we think we are. Barbara Ehrenreich points out in *Bright-Sided* that, "in

*illusion of land of opportunity*

reality, Americans are less likely to move upward from their class of origin than are Germans, Canadians, Finns, French people, Swedes, Norwegians, or Danes." This myth of endless opportunity is just about as valid as the one I believed about my home value being resistant to the force of economic gravity. We don't need to speak truth to power. We need to speak it to ourselves.

*   *   *   *

With a shiver of aversion, I turn off the egotists that dominate so much of our political discourse on the internet, television, and talk radio. They can't seem to participate in a search for truth or even have a civil discussion that would help inform us on pressing vital topics. They are masters at creating doubt about what is really happening, and which path is actually best for us. But these characters and our responses to their performances illustrate how much we have allowed television, talk radio, and the internet to be our experience of the world. Plus, we relegate too much of our personal responsibility to be informed to these sources, and then make value judgments based on them. On the one hand, they stimulate addictions to fear, fight and flight reactions. On the other hand, they invite us to sublimate our anger and our intellects into the weeknight and weekend diversions of late-night comedy shows and independent movies.

These venues turn news into entertainment and make it humorous and fun to satirize our mindless and benighted neighbors and our self-aggrandizing politicians. Both approaches help cause a decline in our ability to thoughtfully take the action our anger and frustration should be leading us toward. The result too often is that our hearts atrophy and are shut away from any great enthusiasms except for private ambition, are shut away from any vision based on the faith that we as a people are more than the sum of our material desires. We should ask ourselves, "How will we be remembered? How will history judge us?" It is so easy to look the other way, to look at our busyness or victimhood. It is tempting, even seductive, to look away from the challenges we are facing.

The propaganda from the predators and self-serving politicians also teaches us that it is easier to see our taxes as a burden rather than an investment in the human and material infrastructure that will benefit us all. It is easier to turn a blind eye to the fact the top one percent of households have more wealth than the bottom 90 percent combined, and it is important and infuriating that one political party seems dedicated to reducing taxes for the wealthy. It is pretty obvious that tax relief for the wealthy never trickles down. It goes into high-yield investments. To increase taxes on the rich is simply common sense—it won't affect their standard of living at all, while increases on the bottom 80 percent significantly affect theirs.

I shudder when I think about asking myself if I am better off than I was thirty years ago. But my anger and disgust have distracted me as I have been writing what is bubbling up. All of the rich, as I have carefully pointed out, aren't predators. However, I want to return to another danger I see in the media: it can make us feel victorious when in fact the battle has only begun. For example, the women's "Me Too" movement is powerful and long overdue. Me Too is terribly important and is having a significant impact. There must never be a time when we fail to have needed protests in our democracy,

*[handwritten margin note: Power of money control]*

but we have to be careful not to congratulate ourselves too quickly because of dramatic media attention. In a December 31, 2017, *New York Times* article, the well-known writer Susan Faludi points out that with all the Me Too publicity going on, the patriarchy hasn't gone anywhere. In fact, in the midst of this publicity, Congress passed the Tax Cuts and Jobs Act, which in Ms. Faludi's words "throws a bombshell on women," young, poor, working class, and older. Passing this law proves further that our democracy is weak. We must all turn our anger into sustained action.

## Rage and Creativity

Oh yes, it has been a rule in my life for a long time that rage is bad. I was taught from the beginning of my life that rage is destructive. For my first ten years or so that teaching was crudely enforced by my father's outbursts of rage, which terrified me even though he was never physically abusive to any of us or even threatened to be. But I sure learned I didn't want to be like him, and I didn't want to scare my children that way. I still have what almost seems like a natural inclination to want to smother my rage even though I now know better.

What does it mean now to know better? It means I have learned that for any real creation, there must be a rage. It takes rage to break through the chrysalis of fear, pride, conventional thinking, our need for approval, or whatever is encapsulating us. Creativity requires the concentration of all our passion, our love, our anger, our rage, and our hatred—the concentration of all of these combined with our sensitivity and our thoughtfulness. This reality is true whether we are creating art, a new business, or a new life.

If we simply act out our rage, we are wasting it in a

destructive manner. Looking back, I want to weep for my father. He expressed his rage over and over. He was wasting it and using it to avoid the real issues. If he had forged it with his other feelings, he could have become passionate enough to break out of the life that encapsulated him and break through the inner barriers of fear that blocked his ability to find his creativity and through it a life with a more satisfying purpose.

We must not waste our rage. And we must remember there are some things we should hate furiously. Acting out rage and hate may bring temporary relief and may make us feel powerful for a moment, but this path is never satisfying in the long run. It can also become a perpetual path of denying the real issues we need to confront. It is much better if we learn how to confront and accept ourselves and forge our rage into the kind of passion and fierce love that fuels creative action.

*  *  *  *

Maya Angelou, the great poet, writer, and educator who inspires me with everything she has said or written, once roared, "Be angry! It is right to be angry. It is healthy!" Well, it is getting very healthy for me. But, I'm not so sure it will be for those who love the status quo, who love peace of mind, who want to avoid life as a creative struggle, and who are afraid of having to confront themselves, their shadows, and the shadows in our government and society.

At this point, my rage is becoming fierce love and tough. It eliminates easy answers, compromises, and considering whether we should follow the politics of the practical. Our country was not founded on this kind of weak thinking. It was founded by people, big and small, who were willing to risk everything. Bobby Kennedy once reminded me of our heritage, saying in his wonderful accent, "Some men see things as they are and ask why. I dream of things that never were and ask why not." These are the words that reflect my belief in the American spirit.

The only way we are going to reclaim the heart of our democracy is to have legislators that are dedicated to the job of governing—not fundraising, personal power, party power, and re-election. The way to have this kind of legislature is clear. First, we have to vote in every election, big and small. We need to have the highest voter turnout of any democratic country. Let's be number one where it counts the most! If you don't like or can't support any of the candidates, write someone else in. Make your protest visible and explicit. Don't sit it out and give an implicit vote to the wrong person. Second, vote for someone totally committed to campaign finance reform. Don't compromise. We must cut the tie between government and personal and corporate wealth or our democracy will fail. Remember, our candidates must deserve us! It must be a privilege for them to serve. Senators and representatives cannot govern when they have to start fundraising and running for re-election as soon as they take office. For God's sake, this is not rocket science, it is simply common sense. Every other politically advanced nation limits campaigns to a few weeks or months and stops them a few days before elections so people have time to collect their thoughts before voting. Elections are not entertainment. They are deadly serious and need to be treated that way.

There are two other hard facts we need to consider. The first one is that we have the right to reform our government every two years in elections. This reforming need not be based on the power politics between the two major parties or the president. It needs to be based on the principles of getting out and voting for campaign finance reform and shortened campaign periods. The second hard fact we have to face is that if we fail to cut the ties between wealth and government, all our concerns about social justice, fairness, women's rights, discrimination, and other problems I have been writing about are causes that will never really get on the table. They will never become more than political tools and lip-service government concerns. We must own our democracy as citizens in order to come together and thrash and hammer these issues into a moral vision that assumes we have a spirit and values higher than our material appetites and economic cravings. We can do this!

Guess what? This 2016 election proved we do have power. The president who was elected, the most unlikely candidate I've ever seen, swept all the well-moneyed traditional candidates in the Republican party right off the board. Bernie Sanders, a Democratic candidate in his seventies, stirred the hearts of the young and young-at-heart who are not trapped in the love of comfort, and almost upset the most well-financed and -engineered campaign I've ever seen in a primary. His message was direct, for the people, and in actuality his agenda was common-sense. Without grand financing or strategies or propaganda, he gathered huge support. This election proves we can do it if we really try with candidates who deserve us.

# THIRTEEN

# THE ROOTS OF
# AMERICA'S GREATNESS

**"** I fear forgetfulness as much as I fear hatred and death," Elie Wiesel declared in his powerful book *From the Kingdom of Memory*. To forget is to deny our origins, our roots, and our people. If we don't know the past, we cannot understand the present or clearly judge how to influence the future. If we are cut off from our roots—our national soul—we will begin to wither and lose our selfhood. Imagine the shocking rage that John Adams witnessed when he saw a Boston tax collector being tarred and feathered shortly before our American Revolution began. This violent outburst by otherwise peaceful citizens was the result of feeling ignored by their government. It shocked John Adams into realizing the need for radical changes in home rule. The rage in our country today should awaken us in a similar way. That rage was the beginning of our national history, and a turning point in western history. If our beginnings are not forgotten, they are not gone; they are still alive today.

Imagine, if you would, those people from the past—
John Adams, Benjamin Franklin, Thomas Jefferson, and
all the others -- gathered in a building in Philadelphia,
struggling to reach the point of adopting a Declaration of
Independence.  They knew they were risking everything,
because if they lost, they would be hung as traitors.  In
that struggle, they gave birth to a challenge that would
shape our history and that of the Western world.

"Freedom, equality, and opportunity" may be
sublime ideas, but they are much, much more than that.
Freedom, equality, and opportunity are needs that were
born out of the soul of humanity, out of the very heart
of humankind—our kind—in the Western world. This
birth took place in the land ruled by the most powerful
king of the age, and in a society where liberty and
equality were not in style.

The courageous people who gave birth to our Declaration of Independence were human beings, like all
of us. They were products of their time and had their
flaws and weaknesses, like all of us. But their example
challenges us to face life with more courage and the
deep desire to fulfill our part in carrying our country's
founding vision a step forward in our lifetime. They did
not create an outline for a perfect world. The Declaration, and our Constitution, reflect some of the human
flaws of those who wrote it, but the moral vision they
created challenges us to meet it, and enlarge it in the
world we are helping to create. The challenge to our
hearts is to remember and carry forward the vision of
"Liberty" married to "Equality" as stated in our Declaration of Independence; and we must remember the
people we elect become the embodiment of who we are.

"We hold these truths to be self-evident...that all
men are created equal, that they are endowed by their

Creator with certain inalienable rights...that among these are Life, Liberty and the Pursuit of Happiness... to secure these rights, governments are instituted among men..." These words also fueled the French Revolution and have brought inspiration to the Western world since they were written. This vision from the soul of humanity should be the backbone of our national life because it is the force that transforms us from subjects into citizens, every one of us. Like our founding fathers, we need to find the greatness of heart and spirit to transcend our fears and weaknesses. If we forget to nourish this taproot in our history, it will die. If we remember it, it lives on, unites us, and empowers our vision of life. It is this vision that has made our nation truly great; admired by the world in a way that supercedes material, economic, and military might.

Remember, with this vision, a bunch of ragged farmers and frontiersmen defeated the strongest government in the Western world at the time. It is our destiny to keep it alive and to fulfill our generation's duty towards it. We must wake up because we who should be tending the flame are in danger of betraying that vision and allowing the flame to be smothered.

## Recapturing Our Challenge for a New Normal

There are four powerful temptations that we must guard against in these fragmented and chaotic times. The first of these is helplessness, the feeling that there is little that I as one person can do against the power, misery, injustice, and violence around me. We are, in fact, able to do something. One committed person can always make a difference. Some of us may cause big changes. Most of us can change a small portion of events. In the totality of all our acts we create the history of our era.

I cannot help but think of all those soldiers during our revolution during the freezing winter at Valley Forge dealing with poor clothing, near starvation, tattered tents and primitive huts for housing, and rampant influenza. At home their wives struggled with taking care of children, elders, farms, shops, and so on. These were mostly uneducated folks, but they understood the needs of the human heart for liberty, equality, and opportunity. They endured. They crossed the freezing Delaware River with George Washington to win a rare victory. They endured for six-and-a-half years, losing almost every battle, until they finally won the war and stood down the army of Lord Cornwallis in a final defeat. This is our heritage. This heritage isn't dead—it tends to drop out of sight until we have a tragedy. I remember with tears in my heart the many police and firefighters who went into the towers on 9/11 knowing they would probably never come out. They proved that deep down our spirit still has the potential to be unconquerable. These men and women remind us of what is best in us. Futility is not an option because every act can create a ripple of hope and change.

The second temptation is <u>practicality</u>. Practicality, expediency, has become far too popular in our times. The idea that we must be practical limits our vision and our possibilities and separates us from the foundational strength of our nation—the strength to rise above ourselves to meet the challenges of our reality and our destiny, to remember that our rights are diminished when the rights of anyone around us are threatened. Theodore Roosevelt taught us by word and deed that only those who dare to fail greatly can achieve greatly. The moral aims and values supported by our visions of liberty, equality, and opportunity for every one of us are not incompatible with the economic possibilities for our society. Capitalism or efficiency without the heart of our value system will lead us to disaster.

(3) The third temptation we have to face is fear. In fact, I am damn sick and tired of having our media and too many of our politicians throwing fear at me all the time. We are the strongest country in the world militarily and economically. I am also sick and tired of the fear we live in due to the ruthlessness of our job markets, our lack of safety nets, and our fear of absurd health-care costs. It is time for us to rediscover the moral courage it takes to reclaim the heart of our democracy. Real freedom and a real sense of personal value in our culture will do a lot to free us from many basic fears. But we have to find the courage our forebears found to start a revolution. Courage is the one essential quality needed to change the world and to gain a life of one's own.

The fourth temptation we face is staying in our comfort zones and following the temptations of easy, familiar paths, whether they are being dependent on public help or following personal ambitions. We can sleepwalk through life, trying to shut out the unpleasantness, and not take self-responsibility for the danger, chaos, and uncertainty in our times. We are the ones who need to step out of our comfort zones and reclaim the heart of our democracy, and the soul of our heritage. We need to be tough enough to follow the example of perseverance shown by the members of our revolution to change our government on the national level, the state level, the county level, and the city level—no matter if it takes six-and-a-half years as our original revolution did. I must also ask if we are tough enough to look in the mirror and say, as the old comic strip character Pogo did, that "We have met the enemy and he is us."

Or I might say it another way: "Do I value myself, my country, and the future I want to see for my children, grandchildren, and the rest of us enough to become fully engaged? Would it also help if I stopped underestimating myself, my power to be engaged, and my potential strength as a citizen?" Sure.

## Daring to Accept Reality And Our Power To Change It

During my lifetime my parents, along with many others living through the Great Depression, committed to create a new reality for our country through the New Deal of President Roosevelt. They began their endeavor by demanding political leadership that recognized something was badly wrong and had the courage and vision to take the country forward. Action and change became their watchwords.

Shortly after the Depression, our country experienced a devastating defeat at Pearl Harbor and in the Philippine Islands that resulted in the terrible Bataan Death March where additional thousands of our service men and women died. My parents and our country responded to this crisis with a full commitment to a shared purpose and direction. With courage and sacrifice in the next four-and-a-half years they changed the history of the world. They changed it again by helping their former enemies rebuild their countries and restructure their futures. Then they changed the world again with the Marshall Plan that helped restore the foundation of war-torn Europe. They were not the perfect generation, but they earned the title of the "greatest generation." This is our heritage in my lifetime. Dare we forget it? This is the heritage of America's strength, "in the ability to stand up to any challenges, no matter how difficult or daunting." Can I, can we, like they did, have the courage to leave our comfort zones, especially those of hatred, ideology, and fear-driven greed, and face the commitment to create a new national reality?

The quest in much of this book is to face the truth of our personal and national reality. A quest Dr. Jung put at the heart of our efforts to become whole and to fulfill the purpose of our lives. This pursuit means facing our shadow, the unpleasant truths about ourselves that we have automatically sought to hide and deny. As a nation we hide behind statistics like the unemployment rate. We hide behind our material success. We hide behind our myths, like everyone has a chance for success through hard work. We hide behind our façade of positive thinking and we hide behind our frantic busyness.

There is no question that we need to make fundamental changes and we need to make them fast. The incremental approach will not bring healing, or civility, or return us to a sense of community. To think we can't change the status of our poor, our sick, and our prisoners (as our great religions instruct us to do) means our fear and regressive impulses are limiting our capacity for creativity, courage, and vision.

Let us be brave enough to tell the truth about global warming. It is a life or death issue! We have a choice: to fully mobilize together to prevent it or to admit we are choosing to participate in causing the greatest humanitarian disaster in history. Every day that goes by without a full commitment to change is another step toward creating a hell for our own grandchildren and all grandchildren to live in.

We are challenged today to become a new great generation – to revitalize our national spirit. We are called to re-ground ourselves in the founding values of our country that initially formed the heart of the American story. This foundation will support us to face and confront the dramatic challenges before us today.

## Thoughts and Questions to Ponder

We are at a turning point in our nation's history and the future is asking us four questions:

- Will we step up to the plate and as citizens reclaim our democratic republic?
- Will we re-humanize our culture by reclaiming our founding values?
- Will we commit ourselves to saving this planet and tomorrow for ourselves, our children, our grandchildren, and humanity?
- Will we claim our heritage and become the next "greatest generation"?

# LIGHT IS ALWAYS BORN OUT OF NIGHT

Heroes and heroines often lost in the woods, faced witches, dragons, dwarves, and trolls in our stories from medieval times. In our complicated age, I, like most of us, have had to learn that as a foundation for change and growth, I have to face dark forces within myself. I have had to learn that there are no new creations without passion, without rage. I am constantly challenged to stay aware of the complexity within myself that shapes how I respond to the events I am experiencing. I take on confronting myself as a personal duty because I care about the world I am helping to create for my children, grandchildren, and the family of humanity.

This is a duty that, while I have tried very hard to fulfill it, I have often failed. Then I am called back to stop, look into my own shadow, my history, my depths, and seek to understand myself better in order to enlarge who I am, and my capacities. There is always an evolving transaction going on between my inner aspects and the forces in my environment. There is constant interplay between me, the person, and me, the evolving member of society.

Any real change in my life involves the breaking up of both my outer world view and my inner world view as I have previously known them. Large or small—any real change brings the loss of some things that gave me my identity and feeling of security. When I have lived through such times, such as my wife's illness, my career changes, my cancer, the recession in 2008, and the 2016 election, there was a time in the middle of the process when I was unable to see the future or trust what it was bringing. Then it seemed as if my natural inclination was to trust what had worked in the past and the traits and values I imagined I possessed.

Yet over the decades and through painful experiences I have learned that it is only when, without bitterness and resentment, I let go of my old vision of who I was and how life should be, and face my shadow that I become free for higher dreams and a greater life. Then, facing the world with its pain and grief opens the door for my creativity and passion to bring new joy and meaning into my life.

\*    \*    \*    \*

My first approach to understanding my situation after the election was to look at myself in my bubble. It surprised me to discover how limited, indifferent, and almost childlike my position was. When I opened myself to the perspective of my dark shadow, I was startled by the aggressive rage and shame that boiled out. My dark shadow added a new level of realism to my outlook, which rang of a deeper truth. At that point, delving into those two positions extensively left me exhausted. When my energy returned sufficiently for me to consider what my golden shadow could contribute, I began to see new opportunities that awakened renewed feelings of hope, passion, and determination in my spirit.

Individually and as a society we must be able to learn from our experience in order to improve. Confronting our shadow is the mechanism for analyzing and understanding our problems, seeing our part in them, and unveiling new possibilities and potentials. We must confront the causes of the anger, hopelessness, alienation, and violence in our society and in our political discourse. We must all be willing to participate in this undertaking—as I am trying to do in this book—to learn from our experiences and improve. We must confront the dark shadow of our social character, the meanness and the cruelty beneath our superficial appearances of success and power, and our belief in the myth that anyone can succeed in this country through hard work and discipline. We must also confront the kind of religiosity that doesn't recognize the infinite potential that God has given us. We are fragmented politically, class-wise and power-wise. The anger and despair that is breaking through our societal persona and the dehumanization of our fellow citizens—not to mention ourselves—and the alienation causing it is growing. We must accept this reality and understand it as the first step in changing it. The second step is reclaiming the heart of our democracy from the wealth and power structures now dominating it.

If we can devote ourselves to this process, we will discover it is in our nature to strive to give form to a better future by recreating and revitalizing the way we are living. While we are in this process, we may also discover that it is a profound act of love to embrace our current reality and let it invite us to take the risks that usher in the promise of a new future.

As I am summarizing my months of reflections and encounters with myself—I have also been trying to follow Dr. Jung's admonition, "… the psychologist cannot avoid coming to grips with contemporary history, even if his very soul shrinks from the political uproar, the lying propaganda, and the jarring speeches of the demagogues. We need not mention his duties as a citizen, which confront him with a similar task. As a physician he has a higher obligation to humanity in this respect."

\*    \*    \*    \*

Thank you for joining me on my difficult journey of awakening.

Bud Harris
Asheville, North Carolina

# A NOTE OF THANKS

Whether you received *The Midnight Hour* as a gift, borrowed it from a friend, or purchased it yourself, we're glad you read it. We think that Bud Harris is a refreshing, challenging, and inspiring voice and we hope you will share this book and his thoughts with your family and friends. If you would like to learn more about Bud Harris, Ph.D., and his work, please visit: www.budharris.com or https://www.facebook.com/BudHarrisPh.D/.

# AUTHOR'S BIO

Bud Harris, Ph.D., is a Jungian analyst, writer, and lecturer, who has dedicated his life to help people grow through their challenges and life situations to become "the best versions of themselves." Originally a corporate business-man, Bud then owned his own business. Though very successful, he began to search for a new ver-sion of himself and his life at age thirty-five. He had become dissatisfied with his accomplishments in business and was being chal-lenged by serious illness in his family. Bud returned to graduate school to study psychotherapy. He earned his Ph.D. in psychology and practiced as a psychotherapist and psychologist for several years. Later, Bud moved to Zurich, Switzerland, where he trained for over five years and graduated from the C. G. Jung Institute to become a Jungian analyst. Bud is the author of fourteen informing and inspiring books. He writes and teaches with his wife, Jungian analyst Massimilla Harris, Ph.D., and lectures widely. Bud and Massimilla are practicing Jungian analysts in Asheville, North Carolina. For more information about Bud's practice and work, visit www. budharris.com or www.facebook.com/BudHarrisPh.D.

Made in the USA
Columbia, SC
23 February 2020